How
Capitalistic
Is the
Constitution?

How Capitalistic Is the Constitution?

Robert A. Goldwin
and William A. Schambra
editors

American Enterprise Institute for Public Policy Research
Washington and London

This book is the second in a series in AEI's project "A Decade of Study of the Constitution," funded in part by a Bicentennial Challenge Grant from the National Endowment for the Humanities. The first book in this series was *How Democratic Is the Constitution?* edited by Robert A. Goldwin and William A. Schambra.

Library of Congress Cataloging in Publication Data

Main entry under title:

How Capitalistic is the Constitution?

(AEI studies ; 348)
"This book is the second in a series in AEI's project 'A decade of study of the Constitution' "—T.p. verso.
Contents: American democracy and the acquisitive spirit /
Marc F. Plattner—Class rule under the Constitution /
Edward S. Greenberg—The Constitution and Hamiltonian capitalism /
Forrest McDonald—[etc.]
1. United States—Constitutional history—Addresses, essays, lectures. 2. United States—Economic policy—Addresses, essays, lectures. 3. Capitalism—Addresses, essays, lectures. 4. Democracy—Addresses, essays, lectures. I. Goldwin, Robert A., 1922— II. Schambra, William A. III. Series.
JK371.S6H74   1982   320.973   81–20624
ISBN 0-8447-3477-2   AACR2
ISBN 0-8447-3478-0 (pbk.)

AEI Studies 348

Printed in the United States of America

Contents

Preface

What is the relationship between free, democratic government and a capitalistic economic system? That is an enduring public issue for the United States. It not only is the source of heated scholarly disputes and protracted political struggles—it also touches all of us in our everyday lives. How we adjust the relationship between government and the economy determines how much tax we must pay, whether we spend or save our pay increases (or whether we get one at all), and whether it is difficult or easy to start and maintain a business or to find and keep a job. In a larger sense, it affects how much freedom and equality we enjoy as citizens and whether our society secures enrichment for the few, or justice for all.

The source of this issue, and therefore the best starting point for consideration of it, and of almost all issues of such magnitude, is the Constitution and the thought of the Founding Fathers. We cannot make a sound adjustment in the relationship of government and the economy today without first understanding what that relationship was intended to be in our founding document and what it has become with time. More important, we may discover in the Constitution and in the thought of the Founding Fathers an understanding of politics and economics as profound as anything we are likely to encounter today.

Consideration of the Constitution is almost always helpful but almost never uncontroversial, as the essays in this volume demonstrate. Some of our authors, for instance, argue that there is a deep contradiction between the democratic, egalitarian promises of the Constitution and the inequalities generated by American capitalism. Others argue that capitalism is not simply compatible with democracy, it is in fact essential for democracy as it was understood by the Founders and as it was established by the Constitution.

Where we stand on that controversy has an important bearing on the way we decide to adjust the relationship between government and the economy today. If capitalism is essential to the American form of democracy, it is possible to argue (as do some of our authors) that we should try to preserve an economic market free of all but minimal political controls and that too much government regulation violates the letter and spirit of the Constitution. If, however, there is a contradiction between capitalism and the Constitution, then the task is to ensure *more* control by the government over the economy, so that inequalities are diminished and the democratic promise is fulfilled.

But are we right to separate the economic and the political as two distinct realms, whether supportive or antagonistic? One of the authors in this volume maintains that the Constitution established a "commercial" not a capitalistic regime, in which no sharp distinction between politics and economics was intended. The Founders, he argues, understood commerce to reconcile a free economic system and prudent political supervision of the economy; if we could recapture that notion of commerce, it would clarify our thinking about the relationship of politics and economics today.

These are some of the issues raised when we ask how capitalistic the Constitution is, and the essays in this volume are designed to give the reader a sense of the importance and complexity of that question. Though the essays answer the question in a variety of ways, they share this assumption: in the American context, there are no important questions that are purely "economic" or purely "political," despite boundaries that have been drawn by academic disciplines. By considering them together, and seeing each inevitably linked and in the light of the other, we acknowledge our debt to the Founding Fathers in the most appropriate way: by attempting to understand, as they did, the task of constituting a nation of free and prosperous men and women.

ROBERT A. GOLDWIN
WILLIAM A. SCHAMBRA

1

American Democracy and the Acquisitive Spirit

Marc F. Plattner

More and more critics nowadays contend that there is a fundamental tension—or even contradiction—between America's capitalist economic order and its democratic political order. The late Arthur Okun opened his influential *Equality and Efficiency* with a discussion of the "double standard of capitalist democracy, professing and pursuing an egalitarian political and social system and simultaneously generating gaping disparities in economic well-being." [1] In a similar vein, Kenneth Keniston, in his foreword to Richard de Lone's *Small Futures*, writes of "the inherent conflict between the inegalitarian consequences of a liberal economy and the egalitarian ideal of a liberal political democracy." De Lone spells out this view at greater length in the book:

> There is . . . a deep tension in liberal thought between the political and economic traditions. The political tradition emphasizes the equal *rights* of all individuals, rights conferred by the natural law from which human reason draws its strength. The economic tradition emphasizes not so much the rights as the *prerogatives* of individuals in the pursuit of self-interest, e.g., the accumulation of property and wealth. Rights and prerogatives often clash. The political tradition of rights embraces equality while the economic tradition of prerogatives leads to inequality. [2]

These critics are quite willing to affirm the democratic character of America's liberal political tradition and its commitment to guaran-

---

[1] Arthur Okun, *Equality and Efficiency* (Washington, D.C.: The Brookings Institution, 1975), p. 1.
[2] Richard de Lone, *Small Futures*, a report of the Carnegie Council on Children (New York: Harcourt Brace Jovanovich, 1979), pp. xi, 28.

teeing equal political rights and liberties to all. They do not dispute the fact that the liberal tradition has historically been associated with support for a capitalist economy. What they do seem to deny is that there is any intrinsic connection between the political system whose protection of equal rights and liberties they applaud and the economic system whose inegalitarian outcomes they deplore. Accordingly, their prescription for the reform of American society consists chiefly of a call for a redistribution of incomes aimed at undoing the inequalities generated by a capitalist economy. They see no danger that such a policy might threaten the liberal political fabric that guarantees our liberties.

I believe that this view derives from a shallow and incorrect understanding of the bases of the American regime, one that overlooks certain critical connections between liberal democracy and capitalism. It is my contention that where the contemporary critics see only an adventitious and ill-matched association, the founders both of liberal political theory and of the government of the United States saw an intimate and indispensable link. In short, I believe that the regime instituted by the Constitution was understood by the framers to be essentially capitalistic. By the equivocal term "capitalistic" I do not mean, in this context, a "free market" economy devoid of any government interference or regulation. Rather, I refer more broadly to an economic system that allows all citizens freely to acquire, possess, and dispose of private property and encourages them to devote themselves to the pursuit and enjoyment of wealth.

The Federalist and the Constitution

For anyone seeking to understand the political and economic thought of the framers of the Constitution there can be no more authoritative source than *The Federalist*. Even Thomas Jefferson, some of whose own views might seem to be in conflict with *The Federalist*, referred to it as a work "to which appeal is habitually made by all, and rarely declined or denied by any as evidence of the general opinion of those who framed and of those who accepted the Constitution of the United States, on questions as to its genuine meaning."[3] Of the

[3] Quoted in Martin Diamond, "The Federalist," in Morton Frisch and Richard Stevens, eds., *American Political Thought* (New York: Charles Scribner's Sons, 1971), p. 52. My understanding of *The Federalist* has been profoundly influenced by Diamond's writings. See also Martin Diamond, "The Federalist," in Leo Strauss and Joseph Cropsey, eds., *History of Political Philosophy*, 2d ed. (Chicago: Rand McNally, 1972).

eighty-five essays that compose *The Federalist*, number 10, in which Publius elaborates his theory of the large republic as the remedy for the diseases of popular government, is widely and justly regarded as the most fundamental.[4] At the heart of his argument appears the following passage:

> The diversity in the faculties of men, from which the rights of property originate, is not less an insuperable obstacle to a uniformity of interests. The protection of these faculties is the first object of government. From the protection of different and unequal faculties of acquiring property, the possession of different degrees and kinds of property immediately results.[5]

This statement—and the critical position it occupies in the all-important argument for the large republic—reveals that the framers of the Constitution recognized that an economic system that permitted material inequalities was not merely compatible with but was an essential aspect of the political structure they sought to establish. It also indicates two other key features of the economic theory that informs *The Federalist*. First, contrary to Richard de Lone's suggestion that the liberal tradition primarily emphasizes economic "prerogatives," Publius speaks here and in several other places of the *rights* of property. Government has the same kind of obligation to protect the rights of property as it does to protect citizens' rights to life and liberty. Second, Publius emphasizes that government is obliged not simply to concern itself with the preservation of property but also to protect people's ability to acquire more of it. The economic theory of *The Federalist* holds that men should be encouraged to exercise to the full extent their "different and unequal faculties of acquiring property," despite the inequality this inevitably produces. A more detailed analysis of *The Federalist's* argument can appropriately begin with the latter point, the encouragement of acquisitiveness and its role in the theory of the large republic that underlies the Constitution.

---

[4] Publius was the pseudonym used by all three authors of *The Federalist*, Alexander Hamilton, James Madison, and John Jay. I refer generally to Publius here rather than to the individual authors of particular numbers of *The Federalist* because I believe that the work as a whole expresses a consistent viewpoint on the issues I am addressing.

[5] Alexander Hamilton, James Madison, and John Jay, *The Federalist*, with an introduction by Clinton Rossiter (New York: New American Library, 1961), no. 10, p. 78.

The Issue of Faction

Federalist 10 is devoted to an analysis of the problem of faction, the "dangerous vice" that has everywhere led to the destruction of popular government. Publius states that there are two ways of remedying "the mischief of faction": "by removing its causes" or "by controlling its effects." And there are, in turn, two ways of removing the causes of faction. The first is the obviously unacceptable expedient of eliminating the liberty that allows factions to grow. The second, which Publius rejects as "impracticable," is to give "to every citizen the same opinions, the same passions, and the same interests." [6]

Stated in this fashion, this alternative sounds utterly unrealizable. Yet the notion that a republic will be happier and freer of faction to the extent that its citizens share a set of common opinions, passions, and interests is not at all implausible. In fact, roughly speaking, this may be taken as the viewpoint of classical political philosophy. Even more to the point in this context, however, is that this is the well-known view presented by Montesquieu in his *Spirit of the Laws,* which is far and away the most frequently cited and discussed work of political theory in *The Federalist.*[7]

According to Montesquieu, the animating principle of republics is virtue. He defines this virtue as "the love of the laws and of our country," and states that it "requires a constant preference of public to private interest." As such, it demands a rigorous restraint of the private passions for pleasure, for wealth, and for personal superiority. Consequently, a well-ordered republic must be characterized by great austerity or purity of morals. Moreover, not only must there be an equality of property, carefully regulated by the laws, but the level of wealth enjoyed by each person should be small: "Since every individual ought here to enjoy the same happiness and the same advantages, they should consequently taste the same pleasures and form the same hopes, which cannot be expected but from a general frugality." Finally, Montesquieu asserts that a republic built on the principle of virtue can subsist only in a small territory, for "in an extensive republic the public good is sacrificed to a thousand private views." [8]

---

[6] Ibid., no. 10, p. 78.

[7] Baron de Montesquieu, *The Spirit of the Laws,* trans. Thomas Nugent (New York: Hafner Publishing Company, 1949). *The Spirit of the Laws* is discussed at length in *Federalist* 9 and 47, and cited in 43 and 78. My analysis of Montesquieu owes a great deal to Thomas L. Pangle's superb study, *Montesquieu's Philosophy of Liberalism* (Chicago: University of Chicago Press, 1973).

[8] Montesquieu, *Spirit of the Laws,* bk. 4, sect. 5; bk. 5, sect. 3; bk. 8, sect. 16; cf. bk. 4, sect. 7.

This Montesquieuan version of republicanism—a small demo-cratic polity characterized by public-spirited virtue, austerity of morals, simplicity and homogeneity of manners, and equally distrib-uted and strictly limited property—is explicitly and emphatically rejected in *The Federalist*. In *Federalist* 9, Publius points out that a strict adherence to Montesquieu's ideas in this regard would require splitting up most of the American states into several smaller polities, which would create "an infinity of little, jealous, clashing, tumultuous commonwealths, the wretched nurseries of unceasing discord and the miserable objects of universal pity or contempt." In *Federalist* 6 he disparages the two most famous historical examples of the virtuous republic: "Sparta was little better than a well-regulated camp; and Rome was never sated of carnage and conquest." In *Federalist* 10 he argues that such small democratic regimes "have ever been spectacles of turbulence and contention; have ever been found incompatible with personal security or the rights of property; and have in general been as short in their lives as they have been violent in their deaths."[9]

In thus rejecting the Montesquieuan model of the small, virtuous, poor republic, however, Publius is in considerable measure following the lead of Montesquieu himself. For after generally praising the ancient republics in the first part of *The Spirit of the Laws*, Mon-tesquieu turns in Book 9 to the issue of political liberty, where he concludes that the general opinion that democracies are the freest form of government is an error, which arises from the fact that "the power of the people has been confounded with their liberty." Political liberty does not consist in the self-rule enjoyed by the citizens of a virtuous republic; indeed, the power such a government exercises over the private lives of citizens places strict limits on their freedom. Montesquieu defines political liberty instead as "a tranquility of mind arising from the opinion each person has of his safety. In order to have this liberty, it is requisite the government be so constituted as one man need not be afraid of another."[10]

Montesquieu takes as the model of such a government modern England, the "one nation . . . that has for the direct end of its con-stitution political liberty." England does not readily fit into the category of either republics (the principle of which is virtue) or monarchies (the principle of which is honor) established in the first part of *The Spirit of the Laws*. Although its political institutions have some republican and some monarchical aspects, it is animated neither by virtue nor by honor. In England, "all the passions [are]

[9] *Federalist*, no. 9, p. 73; no. 6, p. 57; no. 10, p. 81.
[10] Montesquieu, *Spirit of the Laws*, bk. 11, sects. 2, 6.

unrestrained"; the English are "a trading people," who "have ever made their political interests give way to those of commerce." England emerges in Montesquieu's description as having political institutions plainly superior to those of other nations, and especially to the ancient republics. The chief source of this superiority, and the guarantor of its liberties, is the separation it maintains among the legislative, executive, and judicial branches of its government, so that "power [is] a check to power."[11] This separation of powers is, of course, a key element in the new science of politics espoused by Publius, who defends the Constitution's faithfulness to this concept by invoking the authority and the reasoning of "the celebrated Montesquieu."[12]

Having dismissed the possibility of forestalling factions by giving the citizens a common set of opinions, passions, and interests, Publius turns next in *Federalist* 10 to an examination of how the effects of faction can be controlled. In a republic, he notes, regular elections limit the power of minority factions, but they can do nothing to check the potential excesses of a majority faction, that great danger to all popular government. How can a republic be protected from such a faction? The first and most important part of Publius's answer is that "the existence of the same passion or interest in a majority at the same time must be prevented."[13] In other words, far from seeking the greatest possible unity among the citizens, as the legislators of the small, virtuous republic did, the framers of the American Constitution chose precisely the opposite course, of encouraging multiplicity and disunity. Or, as Madison sums it up in a letter to Jefferson that mirrors much of the argument of *Federalist* 10, "*Divide et impera*, the reprobated axiom of tyranny, is, under certain qualifications, the only policy by which a republic can be administered on just principles."[14]

Diversity and Capitalism

The way to achieve the internal divisions required to prevent the formation of a majority faction, Publius contends, is to "extend the

[11] Ibid., bk. 11, sect. 5; bk. 19, sect. 27; bk. 20, sect. 7; bk. 11, sects. 4, 6. At one point, Montesquieu refers to England as "a nation that may be justly called a republic, disguised under the form of monarchy" (bk. 5, sect. 19).

[12] *Federalist*, no. 9, p. 72; no. 47, pp. 301-8.

[13] Ibid., no. 10, p. 81.

[14] James Madison to Thomas Jefferson, 24 October 1787, in Gaillard Hunt, ed., *The Writings of James Madison*, 9 vols. (New York: G. P. Putnam's Sons, 1900), 5:31.

sphere" and thus "take in a greater variety of parties and interests." The large republic founded on the Constitution will embrace "so many separate descriptions of citizens as will render an unjust combination of the whole very improbable, if not impracticable." Simply enlarging the nation's territory, however, will not by itself achieve the requisite diversity unless the different citizens thereby included have genuinely distinct interests. Moreover, since Publius is committed to finding a wholly "republican remedy" to the problem of faction, he cannot rely on that part of Montesquieu's scheme which involves checking the popular interest with those of the nobility and of the monarchy. It is critical to *The Federalist's* concept of the large republic, therefore, that the population be divided into a considerable diversity of *economic* interests. This, in turn, requires a relatively advanced and complex economy. "At present," Publius notes in *Federalist* 56, "some of the States are little more than a society of husbandmen. Few of them have made much progress in those branches of industry which give a variety and complexity to the affairs of a nation." [15] An overwhelmingly agricultural society would not provide the multiplicity of interests essential to the large republic.

Unlike Jefferson, then, who asserts in his *Notes on the State of Virginia* that "the proportion which the aggregate of the other classes of citizens bears in any state to that of its husbandmen, is the proportion of its unsound to its healthy parts." [16] Publius favors the growth of commerce and manufacturing. This preference is visible in many parts of *The Federalist*, but it receives its fullest statement at the beginning of *Federalist* 12:

> The prosperity of commerce is now perceived and acknowledged by all enlightened statesmen to be the most useful as well as the most productive source of national wealth, and has accordingly become a primary object of their political cares. By multiplying the means of gratification, by promoting the introduction and circulation of the precious metals, those darling objects of human avarice and enterprise, it serves to vivify all the channels of industry and to make them flow with greater activity and copiousness. The assiduous merchant, the laborious husbandman, the active mechanic, and the industrious manufacturer—all orders of

[15] *Federalist*, no. 10, p. 83; no. 51, p. 324; no. 10, p. 84 (see also no. 14, pp. 100-101; no. 37, p. 227); no. 56, p. 349.

[16] Thomas Jefferson, *Notes on the State of Virginia*, in Adrienne Koch and William Peden, eds., *The Life and Selected Writings of Thomas Jefferson* (New York: Modern Library, 1944), p. 280.

men look forward with eager expectation and growing
alacrity to the pleasing reward of their toils.[17]

In praising the political utility of commerce, Publius acknowledges
that it prompts men more actively to pursue their private gratification. Far from encouraging public-spirited virtue, it promotes what
traditionally has been considered a vice—namely, avarice. Indeed, the
concern with private gain, Publius later acknowledges, will make the
citizens unwilling to contribute their time to manning the garrisons
necessary to defend their republic's frontiers:

> The militia would not long, if at all, submit to be dragged
> from their occupations and families to perform that most
> disagreeable duty in times of peace. And if they could be
> prevailed upon or compelled to do it, the increased expense
> of a frequent rotation of service, and the loss of labor and
> disconcertion of the industrious pursuits of individuals,
> would form conclusive objections to the scheme. It would
> be as burdensome and injurious to the public as ruinous to
> private citizens.[18]

How, then, can the promotion of commerce and the "pursuits of
gain," which clearly weaken public-spiritedness, redound to the
public good? The first answer, as has been suggested, is that a great
diversity of competing economic interests can supply the foundation
of a free and stable government, provided that those interests are
channeled by properly constructed political institutions. "Neither
moral nor religious motives," Publius argues in *Federalist* 10, "can
be relied on as an adequate control" for the oppressive tendencies of
faction. What virtue cannot be trusted to accomplish, however, the
division of society into a multiplicity of interests can. Such a division
impedes the formation of oppressive majority factions, so that "a
coalition of a majority of the whole society could seldom take place
on any other principles than those of justice and the general good." [19]

In his discussion of the separation of powers, which is also based
on the principle not of restraining the passions but of counteracting
them with the passions of other men, Publius states, "This policy of

---

[17] *Federalist*, no. 12, p. 91.

[18] Ibid., no. 24, p. 161. Publius elaborates on this point in no. 28, pp. 184-85.
That he was aware of the departure this view represented from the classical
republican ideal of the citizen-soldier is revealed in no. 8, p. 69: "The industrious
habits of the people of the present day, absorbed in the pursuits of gain and
devoted to the improvements of agriculture and commerce, are incompatible with
the condition of a nation of soldiers, which was the true condition of the people
of those [that is, the ancient Greek] republics."

[19] Ibid., no. 10, p. 81; no. 51, p. 325.

supplying, by opposite and rival interests, the defect of better motives, might be traced through the whole system of human affairs, private as well as public." [20] He does not specify how this policy operates in private affairs, but he may well have been thinking of the benefits of economic competition, which received their classic exposition from Adam Smith:

> Every individual is continually exerting himself to find out the most advantageous employment for whatever capital he can command. It is his own advantage, indeed, and not that of the society which he has in view. But the study of his own advantage naturally, or rather necessarily leads him to prefer that employment which is most advantageous to the society. [21]

In any event, if increasing national wealth—that is, economic growth—is taken as a desirable political goal, as it clearly is by the authors of *The Federalist*, encouraging individuals to pursue their own private gain becomes a means toward promoting the public good.

Finally, the avarice stimulated by commerce, though undeniably a selfish passion, is nonetheless conducive to habits of industry, prudence, and sobriety—in short, to regularity of morals. [22] Men under the sway of this passion tend to go about their business quietly, seeking gratification in the pleasing reward of their private activities, with little to be gained and much to be lost by disturbing the public tranquility. This self-regulating mechanism makes it possible for government to be relatively unconcerned with the private lives and opinions of its citizens, and to allow them a great measure of personal liberty. At the same time, what Tocqueville called "self-interest rightly understood" leads the citizens freely to support "a government which will allow them to acquire the things they covet and which will not debar them from the peaceful enjoyment of those possessions which they have already acquired." [23]

[20] Ibid., no. 51, p. 322.

[21] Adam Smith, *The Wealth of Nations*, ed. Edwin Cannan (Chicago: University of Chicago Press, 1976), IV, ii, p. 475.

[22] Cf. *Federalist*, no. 44, pp. 281-83.

[23] Alexis de Tocqueville, *Democracy in America*, ed. Phillips Bradley, trans. Henry Reeve, rev. by Francis Bowen, 2 vols. (New York: Vintage Books, 1945), vol. 2, bk. 2, ch. 14, p. 151 (cf. *Federalist*, no. 62, pp. 382-83). The explicit discussion of "self-interest rightly understood" is in Tocqueville, vol. 2, bk. 2, chs. 8-9. I have borrowed the phrase "regularity of morals," used at the beginning of this paragraph, from vol. 2, bk. 2, ch. 11, p. 140. Indeed, the series of chs. 8-20 of vol. 2, bk. 2 of *Democracy in America* provides a marvelously illuminating discussion of the commercial character of the American regime.

Advantages of the Large Republic

The authors of *The Federalist*, then, fully understood that opting for the large republic characterized by representative government, separation of powers, religious toleration, and personal liberty required unleashing the acquisitive or commercial spirit. At this point, it is worth inquiring briefly into the theoretical grounds for their preferring this "modern" alternative to the older ideal of a small republic characterized by direct democracy, religious unity, public-spiritedness, frugality, and economic equality.

In the first place, Publius rejects the classical small republic as "impracticable." Despite their attempts to foster public-spiritedness, unity, and equality among their citizens, regimes supposedly based on virtue have always been afflicted by civil discord: "Theoretic politicians who have patronized this species of government, have erroneously supposed that by reducing mankind to a perfect equality in their political rights, they would at the same time be perfectly equalized and assimilated in their possessions, their opinions, and their passions."[24] In fact, however, men's self-love generally leads them to prefer their private advantage to the public good, and the diversity in their faculties causes them to resist efforts to reduce them to an equality of condition. In particular, men are always inclined to pursue their economic self-interest; hence, despite all efforts to suppress it, a distinction inevitably emerges between rich and poor. Religion and morality are simply too weak to counter—at least over the long run—the human tendency toward self-seeking. The small, poor, virtuous republic is ultimately doomed to failure because it goes against the grain of human nature.

Publius's rejection of the ancient republican model does not seem to derive from considerations of practicability alone, however. The classical political philosophers also were aware of the practical problems posed by men's selfish passions, yet they persisted in their preference for the small, virtuous, poor republic because they regarded virtue not merely as a means toward maintaining republican government but as the end or goal of political life. From such a perspective, it would hardly have made sense to favor a kind of regime that encouraged citizens to pursue their selfish passions. There is almost no evidence of this classical viewpoint in *The Federalist*, however. Publius nowhere suggests that the large republic founded on the Constitution would have as its aim the inculcation of

[24] *Federalist*, no. 10, p. 81.

virtue or piety.[25] Instead, emphasizing the inability of morality and religion to control men's passions, he advocates a set of political arrangements that depends on allowing self-interest considerable liberty. In apparently discarding virtue as a political goal, Publius removes the need for the onerous self-sacrifice and restraint on individual liberty demanded by the classical republic. The ancient republican model thus is rejected for being intrinsically undesirable as well as impracticable.

The Federalist does not offer a systematic discussion of the goals of political life, but where its authors do touch on this great question, they tend to emphasize such ends as security (or safety), liberty, and property.[26] In particular, they echo the thought of John Locke in speaking of the "great principle of self-preservation," the "original right of self-defense," and the violence and uncertainty of men's condition in the "state of nature" which prompts them to "submit to a government." [27] Now, John Locke does of course address this question directly, most conspicuously in the chapter "Of the Ends of Political Society and Government" in his *Second Treatise*. Here he states, "The great and *chief end* therefore, of Men uniting into Commonwealths, and putting themselves under Government, *is the Preservation of their Property*." [28] But Locke also considers the question in a less well known but most revealing passage of his *Letter Concerning Toleration*. This passage, which I shall take the liberty of quoting at length, is preceded by a paragraph in which Locke, after asserting that "every man has an immortal soul, capable of eternal happiness or misery," nonetheless concludes that "the care of each man's salvation belongs only to himself" (that is, it is no business of government): [29]

---

[25] At several places in *The Federalist* Publius does acknowledge that republican government must be based on moral qualities and attachments that go beyond self-interest—see especially no. 49, pp. 314-15, and no. 55, p. 346. Very little is said about how these qualities and attachments may be fostered, however, and their development is certainly not regarded as the goal of the constitutional republic.

[26] Ibid., no. 1, p. 36; no. 3, p. 42; no. 10, p. 78; no. 37, pp. 226-27; no. 85, pp. 521-22.

[27] Ibid., no. 43, p. 279; no. 28, p. 180; no. 51, pp. 324-25.

[28] John Locke, *Second Treatise*, in Peter Laslett, ed., *Two Treatises of Government* (New York: New American Library, 1965), ch. 9, sect. 124. In the sentence immediately preceding the one quoted here, Locke states that he understands the term "property" to include men's "lives" and "liberties" as well as their "estates"; this hardly diminishes, however, the extraordinary political importance Locke gives to property in its ordinary sense of material possessions.

[29] John Locke, *A Letter Concerning Toleration*, ed. Patrick Romanell (New York: Bobbs-Merrill, 1950), p. 46.

But besides their souls, which are immortal, men have also their temporal lives here upon earth; the state whereof being frail and fleeting, and the duration uncertain, they have need of several outward conveniences to the support thereof, which are to be procured or preserved by pains and industry. For those things that are necessary to the comfortable support of our lives are not the spontaneous products of nature, nor do offer themselves fit and prepared for our use. This part therefore draws on another care, and necessarily gives another employment. But the pravity of mankind being such that they had rather injuriously prey upon the fruits of other men's labors than take pains to provide for themselves, the necessity of preserving men in the possession of what honest industry has already acquired, and also of preserving their liberty and strength, whereby they may acquire what they further want, obliges men to enter into society with one another, that by mutual assistance and joint force they may secure unto each other their properties, in the things that contribute to the comfort and happiness of this life, leaving in the meanwhile to every man the care of his own eternal happiness, the attainment whereof can neither be facilitated by another man's industry, nor can the loss of it turn to another man's prejudice, nor the hope of it be forced from him by an external violence. But, forasmuch as men thus entering into societies, grounded upon their mutual compacts of assistance for the defense of their temporal goods, may, nevertheless, be deprived of them, either by the rapine and fraud of their fellow citizens or by the hostile violence of foreigners, the remedy of this evil consists in arms, riches, and multitude of citizens; the remedy of the other in laws; and the care of all things relating both to one and the other is committed by the society to the civil magistrate. This is the original, this is the use, and these are the bounds of the legislative (which is the supreme) power in every commonwealth. I mean that provision may be made for the security of each man's private possessions, for the peace, riches, and public commodities of the whole people, and, as much as possible, for the increase of their inward strength against foreign invasions.

These things thus explained, it is easy to understand to what end the legislative power ought to be directed, and by what measures regulated; and that is the temporal good and outward prosperity of the society, which is the sole reason of men's entering into society, and the only thing they seek and aim at in it.[30]

[30] Ibid., pp. 47-48.

In short, it is Locke's contention that the care and improvement of men's souls—the cultivation of virtue and piety—is not the province of government. Political society is properly concerned only with men's "temporal lives"—that is, their bodily or material existence. What men above all require for their temporal lives are those "outward conveniences" that provide them with "comfortable support." These things are not supplied ready-made by nature, however; they can be acquired only through "pains and industry." The acquisition of "the things that contribute to comfort and happiness in this life," therefore, is naturally men's chief task. But because in the state of nature some men seek to take away the fruits of others' labor, men must unite into political society to achieve the security of their present possessions and future acquisitions on which their well-being depends.

It is easy to see why, in this view of the origin and purpose of political society, "the protection of [men's] different and unequal faculties of acquiring property" might be regarded as "the first object of government." According to Locke, acquiring and enjoying private wealth are the legitimate and reasonable aims of the individual citizen, and hence ensuring the security of these pursuits is the proper task of political society. In this light, the attempt of the small, virtuous republic to impose strict limits on private wealth in the name of the public good is unreasonable, for it contradicts the very purpose of men's entering society—the preservation and enlargement of their possessions.

Although Locke's view of human nature and political society devalues virtue understood as devotion to the common good or as self-sacrifice for the benefit of others, it brings to the fore a particular notion of justice: in essence, that "justice gives every man a title to the product of his honest industry." [31] A man may justly pursue his own self-interested desire for gain to the full, provided he confines the means of that pursuit to "honest industry" and does not seek to deprive others by fraud or rapine of what their own honest industry

---

[31] John Locke, *First Treatise*, in Laslett, *Two Treatises of Government*, ch. 4, sect. 42. Consider the following remarks of Montesquieu on the understanding of justice characteristic of commercial societies: "The spirit of trade produces in the mind of a man a certain sense of exact justice, opposite, on the one hand, to robbery, and on the other to those moral virtues which forbid our always adhering rigidly to the rules of private interest, and suffer us to neglect this for the advantage of others.

The total privation of trade, on the contrary, produces robbery, which Aristotle ranks in the means of acquiring; yet it is not at all inconsistent with certain moral virtues. Hospitality, for instance, is most rare in trading countries, while it is found in the most admirable perfection among nations of vagabonds." *Spirit of the Laws*, 20:2.

has procured. Justice consists in respecting the private rights—and particularly the property rights—of others.

But would not this standard of justice allow industrious men to amass such great riches that their less industrious fellows would be left with none of the "outward conveniences" of life? Locke in effect answers this question in the chapter "Of Property" in his *Second Treatise*. Because "the far greatest part of the value of things, we enjoy in this world" is created by human labor rather than bestowed in fixed proportions by nature, the man of superior industry "does not lessen but increase the stock of mankind." Hence even its poorer members benefit from living in a society that protects and encourages industry; the worst-off Englishman "feeds, lodges, and is clad" better than a "king of a large and fruitful territory" among the Indians of America.[32] Utility as well as justice requires that the rights of property be secure.

The Rights of Property

Providing security for the rights of property is an absolutely central concern of the authors of *The Federalist*. Indeed, Madison, in the letter to Jefferson already cited, suggests that the encroachments of unjust state laws on citizens' rights of private property were the principal factor that led both to the Constitutional Convention and to public readiness to accept "a general reform." [33] *The Federalist* itself is filled with condemnatory references to these problems, specifically attacking state laws that violated private contracts and paper-money measures and more generally deploring the mutability of state laws.[34] It is in these contexts, moreover, that Publius most frequently and emphatically invokes the language of justice and morality: "such atrocious breaches of moral obligation and social justice"; "an accumulation of guilt, which can be expiated no otherwise than by a voluntary sacrifice on the altar of justice of the power which has been the instrument of it"; "practices . . . which have . . . occasioned an almost universal prostration of morals"; "a rage for paper money, for an abolition of debts, for an equal division of property, or for any other improper or wicked project." [35]

The introductory paragraph of *Federalist* 10 alludes to the instability and injustice of state governments, which Publius holds responsible for "that prevailing and increasing distrust of public

---

[32] John Locke, *Second Treatise*, ch. 5, sects. 37, 41.

[33] Madison to Jefferson, in Hunt, *Madison*, 5:27.

[34] In addition to the passages cited in notes 35 and 36 below, see *Federalist*, no. 37, p. 227; no. 44, pp. 282-83.

[35] Ibid., no. 7, p. 65; no. 44, pp. 281-82; no. 85, pp. 521-22; no. 10, p. 84.

engagements and alarm for private rights which are echoed from one end of the continent to the other." In the systematic analysis of the problem of faction that follows, he leaves no doubt that it is the violence and injustice prompted by economic motives that are his chief source of concern:

> The most common and durable source of factions has been the various and unequal distribution of property. Those who hold and those who are without property have ever formed distinct interests in society. Those who are creditors, and those who are debtors, fall under a like discrimination. A landed interest, a manufacturing interest, a mercantile interest, a moneyed interest, with many lesser interests, grow up of necessity in civilized nations, and divide them into different classes, actuated by different sentiments and views. The regulation of these various and interfering interests forms the principal task of modern legislation and involves the spirit of party and faction in the necessary and ordinary operations of government.[36]

Because in a republican government political power naturally comes to reside in majority factions, and because the rich are always in a minority, holds Publius, the greatest danger to property rights is that the poorer members of society may unite to defraud or despoil the wealthy. As we have seen, Publius's principal solution to the problem of faction is to enlarge the territory of a republic to encompass "a greater variety of parties and interests" (by which he appears primarily to mean economic interests). The purpose of this solution is to make the "various" distribution of property more politically salient than its "unequal" distribution. If both the poor and the rich earn their livelihood in a great variety of ways, there will be divergent and competing interests within each group, as well as certain common interests cutting across economic strata. Thus, Publius suggests, poor mechanics will be inclined to vote for the rich merchant as "their natural patron and friend," and a unity of political interest will exist between the "wealthiest landlord" and "the poorest tenant." Furthermore, the extended republic, with its large election districts, would be more likely to choose for its representatives men of "the most diffusive and established characters"—that is, presumably, men of greater wealth.[37] In sum, the large republic is meant to be structured so as to minimize the likelihood that a poor majority will coalesce to violate the property rights of the more prosperous.

[36] Ibid., no. 10, pp. 77-78, 79.
[37] Ibid., no. 35, pp. 214-15; no. 10, pp. 82-83.

The inviolability of the rights of property appears to have been accepted by the full range of American political thinkers of the constitutional era—anti-Federalists as well as supporters of the Constitution, agrarians as well as proponents of commerce and manufacturing.[38] Even Jefferson, despite the notably egalitarian character of some of his views, remained firmly committed to a concept of property rights which promoted and justified unequal material rewards. In his second inaugural address as president of the United States, he affirmed his wish that "equality of rights [be] maintained, and that state of property, equal or unequal, which results to every man from his own industry, or that of his fathers."[39] In a letter to Joseph Milligan, he stated:

> To take from one, because it is thought his own industry and that of his fathers has acquired too much, in order to spare to others, who, or whose fathers have not exercised equal industry and skill, is to violate arbitrarily the first principle of association, "the guarantee to everyone of a free exercise of his industry and the fruits acquired by it."[40]

This is not to deny that Jefferson, along with others of the founding generation, believed that a wide distribution of property, without vastly disproportionate wealth or acute poverty, best comported with republican government.[41] In a letter to the Reverend James Madison (a cousin of his more famous namesake), Jefferson suggests as one "means of silently lessening the inequality of property" the use of progressive taxation, a policy that had been approved by both Montesquieu and Adam Smith.[42] But the principal instrument

[38] See Cecelia Kenyon, ed., *The Antifederalists* (Indianapolis: Bobbs Merrill, 1966), p. xxvii, and E. A. J. Johnson, *The Foundations of American Economic Freedom* (Minneapolis: University of Minnesota Press, 1973), pp. 191-92.

[39] Thomas Jefferson, "Second Inaugural Address," in Koch and Peden, *Jefferson*, p. 344.

[40] Thomas Jefferson to Joseph Milligan, 6 April 1816, in Albert Bergh, ed., *The Writings of Thomas Jefferson*, 20 vols. (Washington, D.C., 1907), 14:466.

[41] See Johnson, *American Economic Freedom*, pp. 310-11. James Madison (in Hunt, *Madison*, 6:86) asserts that republicanism is strengthened "by the *silent* operation of laws, which, *without violating the rights of property*, reduce extreme wealth towards a state of mediocrity, and raise extreme indigence toward a state of comfort" (italics added). The Founders' desire to reduce economic equality is always mitigated by their concern to preserve the legitimate rights of property. Hence they never advocate direct redistributive measures, but seek indirect and unobtrusive—that is, "silent"—means to this end.

[42] Thomas Jefferson to Rev. James Madison, 28 October 1785, in Koch and Peden, *Jefferson*, p. 390. Progressive taxation is endorsed by Montesquieu in *Spirit of the Laws*, 13:7, and by Adam Smith in *Wealth of Nations*, V, ii, Part II, Article 1.

advocated by Jefferson (and others) for preventing inequality of fortune sufficient to threaten republicanism was laws encouraging the equal partition of inheritances. Shortly after the Declaration of Independence was adopted, Jefferson returned to the Virginia Legislature, where he led a successful fight to abolish the laws of primogeniture and entail (which required that landed estates be passed intact to the eldest son). In his autobiography he explains the purpose behind these reforms as follows:

> To annul this privilege, and instead of an aristocracy of wealth, of more harm and danger, than benefit, to society, to make an opening for the aristocracy of virtue and talent, which nature has wisely provided for the direction of the interests of society, and scattered with equal hand through all its conditions, was deemed essential to a well-ordered republic. To effect it, no violence was necessary, no deprivation of natural right, but rather an enlargement of it by repeal of the law [of entail]. For this would authorize the present holder to divide the property among his children equally, as his affections were divided; and would place them, by natural generation, on the level of their fellow citizens.[43]

If Tocqueville's account can be believed, the reformed law of inheritance fully achieved the democratizing effect Jefferson had intended. During the Revolutionary War, almost all the states had abolished the old aristocratic English laws of inheritance; sixty years later, "the law of partition [had] reduced all to one level." By this assertion Tocqueville means that the permanent concentration of vast wealth in certain great families had been eliminated:

> I do not mean that there is any lack of wealthy individuals in the United States; I know of no country, indeed, where the love of money has taken stronger hold on the affections of men and where a profounder contempt is expressed for the theory of the permanent equality of property. But wealth circulates with incredible rapidity, and experience shows that it is rare to find two succeeding generations in the full enjoyment of it.[44]

Results of the Framers' Work

The economic aspects of the framers' political theory may be summarized, then, in the following four points: (1) Industry and the

[43] Thomas Jefferson, *Autobiography*, in Koch and Peden, *Jefferson*, pp. 38-39.
[44] Tocqueville, *Democracy in America*, vol. 1, ch. 3, pp. 49-55.

pursuit of gain should be encouraged. (2) Superior industry and skill justly merit the greater material rewards they naturally tend to reap. (3) The rights of private property must be secured, both on grounds of justice and as a necessary condition for promoting industry. (4) The laws should favor the free and rapid circulation of property, so that all may have a chance to become rich and so that distinct and permanent classes of either the very rich or the very poor are unlikely to form.

The political ends these economic principles were meant to serve are the now traditional liberal goals of liberty and prosperity. National prosperity is the product of individual industry, supported by the security afforded to private property. Liberty is made possible because, given the proper political institutions (representative government, separation of powers, and a large territory), men devoted to industrious pursuits can largely be left to go their own way. The extended republic based on economic self-interest protects the private sphere and gives it unprecedented room to expand. In comparison with the classical republican ideal, the Madisonian version can be said to foster a far-reaching depoliticization of human society. Government no longer need closely supervise the morals, religion, and opinions of the people, for extraordinary public-spiritedness is neither demanded nor needed. The calculating pursuit of economic advantage and the habits of industry provide a check on people's most dangerous and politically destructive passions, and citizens readily give their allegiance to a government that guarantees their liberty and supplies the political conditions they need for prosperity.

I believe it is safe to say that Publius's vision of the large republic animated by economic self-interest has been remarkably successful in bringing the United States almost two hundred years of freedom and material well-being. I believe it is also fair to say that the economic views of the framers, at least as embodied in the principles summarized here, continue to prevail in this country today. To be sure, there have been enormous changes over the past two centuries in technology, in economic organization, and above all in the role played by the federal government in the economy. The modern welfare state certainly goes well beyond anything the framers of the Constitution might have envisioned. And it cannot be denied that the expanded scope of government activity has created difficulties for our political system that have not yet been fully resolved. But whatever the practical problems caused by the proliferation of government programs in the areas of regulation, social insurance, equal opportunity, and aid to the needy, I believe that on the level of principle, the welfare state remains compatible with the liberal capitalist society established by the Constitution—a society that guarantees the security of private property and generally allows material rewards to be allocated according to the "industry and skill" of individuals.

I would argue, however, that proposals for making it an explicit aim of government policy to combat economic inequality directly are a very different matter. In the first place, by focusing on the political competition among income classes (as opposed to that among interest groups formed along other lines), frankly redistributionist policies would intensify the very conflict between the rich and poor that the framers sought to minimize. Moreover, a direct governmental assault on economic inequality would seem to me even more fundamentally incompatible with the basic economic theory underlying the Constitution. It is no accident that the more sophisticated arguments for income redistribution are accompanied by an explicit denial that superior skill or industry conveys a just title to the greater material rewards it normally brings. (This denial is found in Okun's *Equality and Efficiency*, and it is a crucial premise of the most influential work in political theory of the past decade—John Rawls's *A Theory of Justice*.) [45] Having government determine the level of people's income by redistribution can be morally justified only if those who originally earn income have no legitimate right to it.

By making the political process rather than the "honest industry" of private individuals the arbiter of each person's income, redistribution undermines the notion of genuinely private property. For the implicit assumption of such a policy is not that a society's wealth is the sum of the wealth of its individual citizens, but that individuals' wealth is merely the share of the society's wealth that government decides to allot them. By making everyone's income directly dependent on governmental largesse, a policy of explicit redistribution must necessarily politicize society. In effect, each citizen would become the equivalent of a government grantee or a welfare recipient, and it is hard to see how anyone could hope to avoid the government's solicitude about how he or she was spending the public's money. In addition, with everyone entitled to a goodly share of the society's total output, there would be inevitable pressure to regulate the contributions people make to the production of that output. Decisions about whether, where, and when individuals ought to work would tend to become subject to political determination. It seems unlikely, therefore, that a redistributionist society could maintain the

---

[45] Arthur Okun, *Equality and Efficiency*, pp. 42-50; John Rawls, *A Theory of Justice* (Cambridge: Harvard University Press, 1971), pp. 15, 74.

protection of the private sphere necessary for personal liberty to flourish.[46]

One way of describing the error into which I believe the advocates of redistribution have fallen is that they seek to impose on the large republic an economic egalitarianism more appropriate to the small republic. Indeed, I think a very large portion of contemporary hostility to capitalism comes down to a longing for certain attractive features of the small republic—not only economic equality, but intense political participation, a strong sense of community, and selfless devotion to the public good. Few of the contemporary critics of capitalism, however, are willing to sacrifice the blessings of the large, modern, capitalistic republic—unprecedented wealth and personal liberty. Thus they often seem to wind up calling for a utopian combination of contradictory elements—diversity and unity, individualism and community, a high standard of living without resort to the pursuit of private gain. The danger, of course, is that trying to achieve this hybrid in practice will cause us to lose the advantages of the large republic without gaining the advantages of the small republic. In fact, modern totalitarianism can be viewed in some respects as the unfortunate result of just such a misguided attempt.

Lest I be misunderstood, let me hasten to make clear some things I do *not* mean to imply: that the large republic demands an unqualified reliance on self-interest and unbounded libertarianism, that it can or should *totally* dispense with every characteristic of the small republic, or that a capitalist economy is a sufficient condition for political liberty. Indeed, I think the gravest weakness of *The Federalist*'s case for the large republic is its taking for granted the moral and customary props that are essential to the maintenance of self-government in any society. In this respect, an excellent supplement (or corrective) to *The Federalist* is provided by Tocqueville, with his emphasis on the importance of such factors as religion, local government, civil association, and domestic morals to the health of American democracy. Tocqueville constantly stresses, however, the need to adapt these supports to the worldly and commercial spirit of a liberal capitalist society. For he perceived that self-interest—"rightly understood"—was the only reliable basis for political freedom in the modern world.

Certainly the historical record does not reveal any noncapitalist society that has given its citizens a high degree of personal liberty, or any large noncapitalist society that has long maintained a republi-

[46] For a more extended critique of the redistributionist view, see Marc F. Plattner, "The Welfare State vs. the Redistributive State," in *The Public Interest*, no. 55 (Spring 1979), pp. 28–48.

can government. One hesitates, however, to rely too heavily on the evidence of the past in matters like these, remembering Publius's plea in behalf of "the experiment of an extended republic": "Hearken not to the voice which petulantly tells you that the form of government recommended for your adoption is a novelty in the political world; that it has never yet had a place in the theories of the wildest projectors; that it rashly attempts what it is impossible to accomplish." [47] Perhaps a country as large and diverse as the United States could continue to enjoy republican government and personal liberty even if it ceased to have a capitalist economy. This possibility will have to be taken seriously when it comes to be defended with the theoretical insight and persuasive power displayed in *The Federalist*.

[47] *Federalist*, no. 14, p. 104.

2

Class Rule under the Constitution

Edward S. Greenberg

How capitalistic is the U.S. Constitution? To what extent does it support and encourage social and economic relations that may be described as capitalistic and discourage those that are anticapitalistic or noncapitalistic? I believe the Constitution is fundamentally and inescapably capitalistic; precisely how and to what degree, however, is historically contingent and seldom has been closely examined.

By the Constitution I mean more than simply the written document. Although the express provisions of the document form the bedrock of any definition of it, a real understanding of the Constitution also must include the authoritative interpretations added over the years by Congress, the president, and the Supreme Court. To this I would add longstanding institutional practices and widely shared political traditions in the United States. By this broad (though hardly unusual) definition, the Constitution is clearly capitalistic. Except in times of instability and revolutionary upheaval, the dominant institutions in any society tend to be congruous and mutually supportive. The social arrangements, distributions of power, and prevailing ideas that characterize the political, economic, and cultural domains generally reinforce one another. Indeed, one of the key indicators of emerging tensions and potential disruptions to normal processes in any polity is the appearance of serious divergence among these domains. To claim that the U.S. Constitution is basically capitalistic, then, when it is the constitutive document of the world's leading capitalist nation, is no radical statement. What would be far more surprising—and would require far more justification—would be to claim that the constitutional-legal order and the prevailing economic arrangements in the United States are different, unrelated, or hostile to each other. Such a situation would make for a strange society indeed, and, as far as I am concerned, an untenable one.

By assuming the Constitution to be capitalistic, I do not mean to suggest that it is constant and fixed. On the contrary, the flexibility and adaptability of the U.S. Constitution have been cited so often that they have become one of the enduring clichés of American life. What is remarkable about the Constitution is that it manages to be both fixed and flexible at the same time. The document's constancy is its commitment to support, encourage, and nurture an economy based on private property. Its adaptability and flexibility grow out of its need to meet this fixed commitment in radically contrasting environments—environments created largely by the transformative qualities of a dynamic capitalism. It is this combination of constancy and adaptability in the American constitutional tradition that lies at the heart of its relationship to a capitalist economy.

To comprehend the fixed character of the Constitution, one must understand the nature of the capitalist state, as well as the relationship of the fundamental law to such a state. To comprehend the flexibility of the Constitution, one must come to grips with the ability capitalism has shown to transform society, as well as to transform itself from something approximately laissez faire in the early nineteenth century into its present concentrated corporate form; and one must understand how the Constitution has adjusted to these drastically altered circumstances. The Constitution has managed to adapt, I believe, by helping to provide a relatively stable context within which different fractions of capital, with different immediate interests and different long-term conceptions of the proper role of government in a capitalistic order, have been able to join in the struggle for dominance. As a document of flexibility, the Constitution can be interpreted as a complex institution that helps define the legitimate boundaries of intracapitalist political struggle and record its outcomes.[1]

The Marxist Theory of the State

Understanding the Constitution requires, first of all, a theory that makes sense of the general nature of the capitalist state—a theory that in particular addresses the origins, purposes, operations, and effects of governmental and political institutions. Several partially developed theories of this sort are familiar to Americans. Free-market conservatives such as Milton Friedman, James Buchanan, and William Simon generally view government as the result of a contract drawn among individuals for the purpose of protecting their individual rights, property, and the public order, and blame the increasingly

[1] The Constitution is also reflective of the outcomes of *inter*class struggles, but that is the subject of another paper.

illegitimate, excessive, and ill-advised activities of the federal government on the politics of special interest, entitlement, and egalitarianism. Reform liberals from Franklin Roosevelt to Edward Kennedy generally have viewed government as the institution that smooths the rough edges of capitalism; standing between classes, as it were, and without interests of its own, government serves as the unselfish instrument of the general welfare. Pluralist thinkers from Robert Dahl to David Truman also view modern capitalist governments as divorced from any particular class, but they see overall public policy as the product of continually changing temporary coalitions that exist in any complex, democratic polity. All these positions, whether they applaud or deplore the present political-economic situation, share the view that the state is both disinterested (not tied to a particular social group or class) and democratic (the product of popular aspirations and liberal-democratic political machinery).

It is my view that although each of these positions points to some partial truths, none of them adequately helps us to understand the meaning of modern government in the United States. What I propose in their stead is another theory of the capitalist state, and thus of law and constitution—one that is derived from Marxian social and political theory.

From this perspective, all societies are divided into classes in that one section of the population owns or controls the means and purposes of production and organizes the labor power of the vast majority of the remainder. At the center of every society, therefore, is a basic antagonism which—whether people are conscious of it or not—makes class struggle the central dynamic in any mode of production. Under normal conditions, this division takes the form of domination and subordination. The owners or controllers of the means of production are dominant over the whole of society. Their domination takes several forms. Economic domination is the most obvious and need not detain us. Marx also suggested that the class that owns the means of material production sees its own ideas, perspectives, and biases translated into the dominant modes of thought for the entire society. Finally, and largely because of its domination of the society's economic and ideological life, this class also dominates virtually all the complex machinery of government. Thus, in the classical period the state was the organizational expression of slave owners' need to keep slaves in their place; and in our own era, representative government is the instrument capital uses to exploit wage labor.[2] Government is the means by which dominant

---

[2] Many Marxists also view Soviet-style societies as class divided, with the state the expression of the division.

economic actors protect their position against real or potential threats.

Some of those threats come from the downtrodden classes; others emanate from impersonal economic forces. Under modern capitalism, the dominant class needs the state because by itself this class cannot, given limited time, skills, and resources, do everything necessary to maintain its own domination. This class is rendered less effective than it might be because of the intense competition among capitalist enterprises in the economic arena, an unstable and dangerous situation that requires an institution to serve the universal interests of the class rather than the particular interests of any enterprise or group of enterprises. To the extent that this function is not already carried out as a matter of course in the normal operations of material production and by the socializing power of the prevailing ideology, the class requires agents to (1) help maintain the division of classes; (2) co-opt, deflect, or crush threats to prevailing property relations; and (3) regulate social and economic life so as to protect the distribution of benefits and advantages that flow to the dominant class from the processes of production. Marx summarizes the interrelationships among production, class relations, and the state as follows: "The bourgeoisie pay their state well and make the nation pay for it in order to be able without danger to pay poorly."[3]

The state then, is both an expression of the basic tension in the social relations of production derived from class division and the instrument that eases that tension and prevents the full expression of the class struggle. The state becomes a principal means of protecting and reproducing the overall system, for it is the guarantor of the conditions for continued production and reproduction. It is an aspect of class relations; yet it also masks and disguises the reality of class antagonism. Though it is at all times either the direct instrument of the economically dominant class or the protector of class society in general from which the dominant class benefits, the state is a political institution which speaks in universal terms in the name of the "general interest" of the "nation-people" and all its classes. The state is the instrument of a particular class parading around, as it were, under the banner of universality.

This is but a simplified model—the formula version, if you will— of the capitalist state as articulated in Marxian theory. As with any scientific model, its simplicity is both its strength and its weakness. Working models have the obvious advantage of cutting through non-essentials, but at the cost of complexity, richness, and nuance. This

---

[3] Karl Marx and Frederick Engels, *The German Ideology* (Moscow: Progress Publishers, 1964), p. 216.

general problem has been a particular problem with the Marxist model in that, either because of misreadings of his work or because of deliberate distortions, social scientists and political commentators have tended to see Marx's work as deterministic, closed, and final. Marx's theoretical analysis has been construed as postulating almost mathematical relationships between economy, society, and state, though in fact no such rigidity characterizes it. I will not review Marxist literature here, but it is important that I briefly mention a set of caveats and distinctions in Marx's theory of the state that are essential for understanding the role of law and constitutions in modern capitalism.

First, although Marx conceptualized general historical laws and tendencies, he insisted that real societies be understood as historically specific entities that vary within those laws according to their own unique circumstances. Thus, although the Marxian tradition takes the general relationship between class and state as given, it views the particular form of state activity in any situation as dependent upon historical settings and circumstances, the form and health of the economic system, and the particular constellation of class forces.

Second, although the state in the Marxian view is an instrument of the dominant class, its every activity need not directly serve class functions. It also carries out operating functions necessary to all societies. Thus the capitalist state always has a dual character. On the one hand it is an instrument reflecting, in concentrated form, the needs of an economically dominant class faced with the continual problems of accumulating capital and pacifying the subordinate class. In these realms, state activities range from providing subsidies to making an ideological defense of property to overseas expansion to strikebreaking. On the other hand, the state also performs certain functions necessary to meet collective needs, such as providing sanitation, public health, public order, disaster relief, and defense.

Third, a given state's activities are determined less by the direct command of a unified dominant class than by the configuration of the class struggle in that society. By its nature, class struggle is never static. It reflects a reality that is always in tension, conflict, and flux. Nor is a society ever composed of two internally unified and opposed classes; rather, classes vary over time, both internally and in the degree to which their opposition to each other is manifest. Government policy and activities, then, far from being a simple expression of the dominant class's interests, are shaped by a complex class struggle which has both interclass and intraclass components and which may change substantially over time.

Finally, any "simplistic" class analysis of the capitalist state is belied by the fact that in order to maintain and reproduce the system as a whole government must respond not so much to the commands of the dominant class but to the tensions and contradictions that threaten the stability of the system. The state in capitalism, according to Nicos Poulantzas, is that institution that serves as the element of global equilibrium in the social system.[4] In this view, government is not a product of direct manipulation by the ruling class so much as an institution responsive to the contradictions and constraints of the capitalist system of production. As such, the capitalist state is always autonomous: To fulfill its task of perpetuating and reproducing the system as a whole, it must often operate apart from the dominant class, and occasionally must act counter to that class's short-term interests. The degree of state autonomy is, of course, historically contingent. Indeed, one of the enduring dramas of government in the United States is the conflict between the state's role with respect to narrowly based interest groups and its role as general coordinator and protector of corporate capitalism as a whole, with first one role and then the other in ascendancy.

From Marxian social theory, then, we can come to an understanding of the capitalist state in which government is an institution that attempts to maintain the system of unequal distribution of power and benefits and thereby advances the general interests of the owners of the means of production. Contrary to the conventional interpretation advanced by those who fail to comprehend Marx's underlying theory, the state is far more than a superstructural (and therefore unimportant) derivative set of institutions. Rather, it is vital and irreplaceable, necessary to the continuation of economic society. The particular forms taken by the capitalist state and the specific content of its public policy, however, are historically contingent, depending on economic developments, interclass and intraclass relations, and political alignments within a given society. All these distinctions come into play when we look at capitalism in relation to the Constitution.

Marxist Theory of Law

Law, whether public or private, statutory or constitutional, is the product of governmental action of one kind or another. In the Marxian view, therefore, it can be understood only in the context of a theory of the state. If we assume that capitalist society is a class society in which the state broadly serves the interests of the

[4] Nicos Poulantzas, *Political Power and Social Classes* (London: New Left Books, 1969).

27

capitalist class, then the law is simply one among several instruments that help the state maintain the conditions of capitalism.

Law is all too often interpreted as something mystical, holy, and transcendent, the glue distilled from generations of human history which holds civilized society together and frees it from the terrors of both arbitrary tyranny and anarchy. Yet law is a human construct, fashioned out of the perceived needs, interests, and actions of particular groups of individuals. Invariably, these groups are the same ones that dominate society in general. The body of law, then, reflects the social order and becomes a codification of the character-istic relationships that prevail in a particular society. The law places the power of the state behind the rules and practices that govern everyday social relations.

Historically, the social relations to which the law and the state give substance generally have been those between unequal classes. In feudal society, lord and serf faced each other as unequal persons and over time worked out customary ways of relating to each other economically, socially, politically, and religiously. In time, these relationships came to be codified in laws which specified the rights and obligations of each party. In capitalist society, the law has come to embody the domination of property over wage labor.

There is no mystery about this. Law is primarily the creation of public institutions (legislatures, executives, and courts), all of which are largely under the control of the dominant class and solicitous of its general and sometimes specific interests. Nor is this view a particularly radical one; it has long been accepted even by theorists friendly toward a free-market view of society. Adam Smith once pointed out that "till there be property there can be no government, the very end of which is to secure wealth, and to defend the rich from the poor."[5]

Law, in short, is one of the means by which those groups that dominate a society, its economy, and its government legitimate and solidify their position. Law is necessarily consistent with prevailing social practices and relations; if it were not, the society would be in a state of revolution.

The Constitution and Fixed Commitments to Capitalism

There is a tendency to overstate the significance of the Constitution in American life. I believe it would be appropriate to deflate our idea of the scope of the power and effects of the U.S. Constitution—or

---

[5] Adam Smith, *An Inquiry into the Nature of Causes of the Wealth of Nations* (Chicago: Encyclopaedia Britannica, 1952), p. 311.

any constitution, for that matter. In the Marxian view, law and constitutions operate within boundaries set by the prevailing system of class relations. Non-Marxist scholars sometimes have arrived at the same conclusion, though by different routes. Robert Dahl, to take the most important case, has argued in a classic study that polyarchy is preserved not by constitutional provisions but by the pluralistic character of American society; that the United States is democratic (in the pluralist sense) not because the Constitution is democratic but because American society is democratic.[6] I would put it somewhat differently: The United States is not capitalist because of the Constitution, the Constitution is capitalist because the United States is capitalist.

This is not to say, of course, that the Constitution is without importance or that it does not affect the behavior of political actors. Constitutions, after all, do specify the organization of political institutions and the distribution of relative powers among governing bodies. No constitution, however, can independently change the purposes and commitments of the capitalist state. Constitutions simply specify which institutions will fulfill state purposes.

The overall functions of the capitalist state fall into three categories: accumulation, legitimation, and repression. By "accumulation" I mean those governmental activities related to the creation and maintenance of conditions in which business enterprises can operate profitably and expand their operations. "Legitimation" refers to those activities that help to incorporate subordinate and potentially disruptive and revolutionary groups into the prevailing social order. "Repression" refers to those activities with which government forcibly prevents the political expression of anticapitalist tendencies when legitimation fails. The Constitution helps define the institutional framework for each of these activities.

Activities related to accumulation are the most obvious and most often discussed, even by non-Marxist scholars, so they need not detain us. Let it suffice to point out that whatever controversies are still going on over the Constitutional Convention, scholars seem generally to agree that virtually all the delegates who attended were committed to setting up conditions that would protect property of all kinds against "leveling" tendencies, and would give the acquisitive spirit full rein. The Founders were remarkably successful in these purposes, and the accumulation functions of the state have continued to expand and be refined over the years. To be sure, democratic

---

[6] Robert A. Dahl, *A Preface to Democratic Theory* (Chicago: University of Chicago Press, 1956).

tendencies have significantly altered some aspects of the Constitution. The work of the Constitutional Convention remains impressive, however, for the stable political structure it established—slow to respond to temporary popular majorities, abundant in "veto points" available to powerful interests, yet flexible enough to allow for changes in policy in the face of determined need on the part of business. This flexibility can be seen in the way the role of government has been transformed from policeman of the business order to general nurturer, encourager, and stimulator of business. Without reviewing the constitutional amendments, court interpretations, institutional practices, and legislative mandates that have comprised the transformation, one can see how the capitalist state today helps to advance the interests of the class that controls production by activities as diverse as granting business subsidies and loan guarantees, managing the business cycle (with decreasing effectiveness), allowing for extensive business self-management under government auspices, protecting quasi-cartels through regulatory agencies, providing an environment of relative labor peace through formalized collective-bargaining procedures, protecting the overseas activities and investments of American-based multinational corporations, and subsidizing business's essential infrastructure (for example, manpower-training and research-and-development programs). Although some of the details have changed through the years, the role of government as a principal prop of business civilization remains firmly established.

The accumulation functions of the state are overt and obvious. The legitimation functions are more subtle, yet they are equally important in establishing the capitalistic nature of the Constitution. To be sure, the legitimation of capitalism in general, as Antonio Gramsci has observed, takes place primarily outside the domain of the state, in what might be called civil society.[7] In the industrialized Western nations, the domination of capital is based primarily on what Gramsci termed *hegemony*—consent that is the product of the spontaneous loyalty dominant groups gain by virtue of their social and intellectual prestige, their leadership of productive and political life, and, conversely, the resignation and confusion their subordinates derive from being dominated. Nevertheless, the state is more than an instrument of coercion; it does have a role in legitimation. A stable political order cannot rest on force alone but must appear legitimate to the people who constitute the political community. All ruling elites,

---

[7] Antonio Gramsci, *The Modern Prince* (London: Lawrence and Wishart, 1975); idem., *Letters from Prison* (New York: Harper & Row, 1973); idem., *L'ordine nuevo* (Turin: Einaudi, 1954).

whatever the form of government, therefore lend considerable effort to enhancing their legitimacy. The United States cannot and does not escape this logic. The Constitution contributes to this objective in several ways.

First, as political scientist Ted Lowi has so ably pointed out, the very act of writing a constitution is an open bid for the consent of the governed.[8] The writing of a constitution is surrounded by the symbolism of a *founding*, an event that establishes a political order characterized by both the exercise of human reason and a strict delimitation (normally) of the powers of the state. Such an event makes the establishment of the political order seem more than a simple seizure of power. The symbolic power of the founding gains a transcendent air from appeals in both the document and the commentaries surrounding it to the most exalted values honored in the society (democracy and liberty in the U.S. Constitution, revolutionary socialism in the Soviet Constitution, Islam in the present Iranian Constitution, and so on). The constitutive mechanism, in short, if it is successfully executed, contributes an air of impartiality and ties the state to deep-seated and widely honored values. To the extent that the state in fact advances the interests of a particular group (the ruling party bureaucracy in the Soviet Union, the capitalist class in the United States), the symbolic aura surrounding the constitution making serves to obscure that reality and forge a powerful instrument of consent.

Second, the U.S. Constitution is an important instrument of legitimation in that it helps to obscure the class relations at the heart of the society. It does this in a number of ways, but most importantly by simply being silent about social classes—by banishing them from view in government and political processes. This silence takes two forms. On the one hand, the Constitution speaks in universal terms of community, commonality, and "people-hood" rather than in terms of groups and classes. The state is presented as the manifestation of national unity ("We the People"), the embodiment of the citizenry as a whole, undivided by material interests. On the other hand, the Constitution relates to people as free and equal citizens, as isolated actors without connection to social classes. The rights and obligations of citizenship are attached to each person as an isolated being, although in life outside of political society, each is tied to a class defined by economic relations. The whole effect, then, is that citizens see themselves in the reflection of the Constitution as part of mass society, not class society.

---

[8] Theodore J. Lowi, *American Government: Incomplete Conquest* (New York: Holt, Rinehart & Winston, 1976), p. 91.

In general, liberal representative democracy has this tendency to separate the economic from the political. Indeed, this is a central characteristic of the capitalist state. As Poulantzas has observed:

> The capitalist state presents this peculiar feature, that nowhere in its actual institutions does strictly political domination take the form of a political *relation* between the dominant *classes* and the dominated classes. In its institutions everything takes place as if the class "struggle" did not exist. This state is organized as a political unity of a society of divergent economic interests and these are presented not as class interests but as the interests of "private individuals," economic subjects: this is connected to the way in which the state is related to the isolation of socioeconomic relations.[9]

Finally, a few words are in order about the repressive functions of the capitalist state. Given limitations of space, I will simply advance a few points about repression that most people will find, if not comfortable, at least reasonable.

First, any government can be viewed as an institution of authoritative coercion. Second, the various instruments of coercion are rarely, if ever, exercised at random, but are used in some systematic way. In the United States, the instruments of public order have been directed almost exclusively against persons and groups who are perceived to represent threats to the prevailing capitalist order. Third, repression in America is unusual in that it is not the province of any single identifiable institution (there is no KGB or its equivalent). Rather, it is characterized by complex instruments and decentralized control of those instruments, which are scattered among various branches of federal, state, and local governments, as well as private individuals and groups. The Industrial Workers of the World, to take one case, met repression not so much from the federal government as from state governments, local police, and vigilante groups. Should the occasion arise, however, I have no doubt that the federal government would move to fulfill its constitutional mandate to "insure domestic tranquility." Repression is in reserve, necessary only when legitimation processes prove insufficient to guarantee the stability of the capitalist system.

Capitalist and Constitutional Transformation

To argue that the Constitution is firm in its support of capitalism, as I have mentioned, is not necessarily to argue that it is unbending

[9] Poulantzas, *Political Power and Social Classes*, p. 188.

32

and inflexible. On the contrary, it is precisely the Constitution's ability to permit timely innovation in the face of dramatic transformations in economic society that best accounts for its historic staying power. While remaining capitalistic at its core, the Constitution has usually (though not invariably) allowed room for creative maneuver as different fractions of capital have vied for economic supremacy and for the opportunity to place their stamp on public policy. Thus, although capitalism is enshrined in the Constitution, no one particular form of capitalism is enshrined.

The fluid character of the Constitution, then, allows it to accommodate not only to pressures from below on occasion but also to struggles between different fractions of the capitalist class. That class, despite its common commitment to the protection of private property and the free market (which represents its unity vis-à-vis the working class), is internally divided by type of business activity (mercantile, industrial, or finance capital), size, market position, and region of activity. The economic struggle among these various groups is mirrored in political struggles over public policy. Constitutional and political practice shifts accordingly, in the long run, accommodating (though often with serious time lags) to the prevailing configuration of economic and political power.

This process of accommodation, which has been going on since the Constitution was ratified, is worth reviewing. Accordingly, I shall describe the broad outcomes of what I see as the three major historical phases of intracapitalist economic and political struggle, and relate these outcomes to changes in the Constitution and the political system. Given limitations of space, my analyses of these periods will be brief.

1789 to 1865. Rather than enter the dangerous lists where scholars have long been engaged in bloody battle over the origins of the Constitution, I shall start with the long period stretching roughly from the ratification of the Constitution through the Civil War. This period opened with a precarious compromise among various capitalist property interests, moved into an interval of struggle among them for supremacy, and ended with the triumph of one of them in both economic and political terms.

In the late eighteenth century, the Constitution represented a tenuous accommodation between landed capitalism based on slavery (yet commercially oriented) and an emerging and dynamic capitalism based primarily but not solely on trade and small manufacturing. Those in both camps seem to have agreed that union and order were preferable to anarchy and the threat of impassioned antiproperty majorities. The debates surrounding the writing of the Constitution and its ratification were never between capitalist and noncapitalist interests, between capitalism and feudalism, or between capitalism and socialism. Neither feudalism nor socialism were on the agenda in Philadelphia because the American colonies were generally capitalistic in mood and organization from the beginning, being tied by culture, by arms, and by economics to an emerging capitalist world power in England.[10] Furthermore, the colonies were populated by eager entrepreneurs and situated far away from any viable competing systems of social organization. Although a panoply of debate surrounded particular provisions of the Constitution, its essential capitalist character was axiomatic. On this the main fractions of the property-owning class were in full agreement.

The precarious compromise among those fractions was exploded by the dramatic transformations in economic life and organization that took place in the first half of the nineteenth century. In the late eighteenth century, most American business activity was accounted for by trade, investments in land, and the sale and use of slaves. By 1807, overseas trade had expanded rapidly, fueled by the orders of the warring European powers. By 1830, the great trading houses that had arisen during the boom began shifting investments from external to internal ventures, particularly in transportation, banking, and manufacturing. By about 1850, financed directly by merchant capital or indirectly by it through the increasingly important investment banks, industrial capitalism had emerged in vigorous, though infant, form. In that year, the "value added" by manufacturing had already exceeded 50 percent of all agricultural production; the railroad, the sewing machine, and the reaper were in widespread use; large factories had appeared; and a sizable industrial proletariat had entered upon the historical stage. In short, capitalism in the Northern states had reached the take-off point for its subsequent leap into full-scale industrial capitalism.

Capitalism in the Southern states, on the other hand, remained mired in stagnation. Based as it was on slavery, vast landholdings, and aristocratic economic, cultural, and political hegemony, it was never able to discard its precapitalist, premodern economic impediments.[11] Plagued by the absence of a home market, low labor pro-

[10] By 1780, the enclosures were completed in England, agriculture was dominated by market-oriented farmers utilizing hired labor, and the great textile mills of the midlands were in full blossom, their looms manned by a vast population of depressed "free" labor.

[11] As Barrington Moore, Jr., has put it, "The South had a capitalist civilization . . . but hardly a bourgeois one." *The Social Origins of Dictatorship and*

ductivity, technological backwardness, and depleted soil, the slave-holding South was rapidly eclipsed economically by the dynamic capitalism of the Northern states. With its way of life under siege, economically threatened yet led by a relatively cohesive and politically astute ruling class, the South pursued strategies of expansion into the West and opposition to federal measures designed to further the interests of Northern capitalism (particularly the tariff). The clash between the two capitalisms, one forward-looking and dynamic, the other backward-looking and stagnant, was perhaps inevitable, and the ultimate results predictable.

For the only time in American constitutional history, capitalist fractions were unable to settle their differences peacefully. Perhaps this was because their differences were irreconcilable; perhaps it was because the exploited class that might have forced their alliance by opposing them was too immature to represent a tangible threat; perhaps it was because competing ways of life were at issue.[12] The Civil War was the outcome of their failure, the ultimate and terrible conclusion to their struggle, and the only case when the Constitution proved inadequate to its mandate. Out of that intracapitalist struggle, merchant-industrial capitalism emerged supreme. Out of the shambles of the Civil War arose an economic society characterized by free enterprise, industrialization, the market mechanism, and commodicized ("free") labor, with the economic and political power of landed and slave capital erased forever from the United States.

The economic struggle between these capitalist fractions and the eventual triumph of merchant-industrial capital were mirrored in a wide range of alterations in constitutional and political practices during this period. I shall mention only the most significant development here. First, the Marshall Court made important contributions to the creation of a national market economy. Chief Justice John Marshall was a strong believer in the Hamiltonian doctrine that American greatness would be constructed on an alliance between a strong central government and a vigorous private-enterprise sector. In keeping with this doctrine, Marshall helped fashion a series of landmark decisions which helped to free business from the restraints of state governments, strengthened the federal role in interstate commerce, and helped to construct an open, vital national market economy. The cases are familiar and need not detain us.

Democracy (Boston: Beacon Press, 1966), p. 121. The same point is elaborated by Eugene Genovese in *The Political Economy of Slavery* (New York: Pantheon Books, 1965).

[12] The point cogently made by Genovese, ibid.

Second, the first half of the nineteenth century saw a significant upsurge in governmental promotion, protection, and subsidization of business activity, particularly in trade and manufacturing, and particularly in the Northern states. The federal government played a role, contributing tariffs to protect infant industry, naval protection, and consular services on behalf of international trade, but it was the state governments that were most active. Before the Civil War, state governments were responsible for about 70 percent of all investments in canals, and 30 percent of investments in railroads. The states also granted generous favors to business, ranging from the funding of vocational training to the loosening of the laws of incorporation to policies of noninterference in the conditions of labor (except for occasional strikebreaking and timely passage of anti-union conspiracy laws).

Third, the first half of the nineteenth century witnessed a dramatic transformation in private law. The central change, which Morton Horwitz has brilliantly described, was the gradual victory of one kind of property use over another.[13] This practical transformation involved a change in the meaning of property itself, from the relatively static notion that an owner was entitled to undisturbed enjoyment (a view most compatible with landed capital) to an emphasis on productive use and development (most compatible with merchant-industrial capital). Other developments in private law were equally dramatic, including the gradual disappearance of the notions of "just price" and inherent fairness in contracts, as well as many traditional protections for hired labor. By 1850, Horwitz argues, the private law represented a bulwark for an emerging, dynamic free-enterprise economy.

Fourth, and perhaps most important, the economic and military victory of the free states over the slave states—the victory of merchant-industrial capital over landed capital, if you will—was established concretely in the Constitution by the Thirteenth, Fourteenth, and Fifteenth Amendments, which erased the slave system and confirmed "free" labor as the prevailing form of material production in the United States. All future intracapitalist debate and class struggles would be joined on this terrain.

The Late Nineteenth Century to World War II. With the dominance of industrial capitalism firmly established by the last third of the nineteenth century, the prevailing forms of the class struggle changed.

---

[13] Morton J. Horwitz, *The Transformation of American Law, 1790–1860* (Cambridge: Harvard University Press, 1977).

The cause was the rapid advance of production, the appearance of large factories and urban concentrations, and the rise of the modern corporation, all brought about by the industrial and organizational revolutions. The most obvious result was the first serious, sustained, and organized struggles in the United States between wage labor and capital. That story is a familiar one. The other struggle, less familiar but more central to this discussion, took place *within* the capitalist class, between small and medium-sized regional businesses on the one hand and the giant national corporations on the other. That struggle was twofold, fought in the economic sphere for shares in the market-place and in the political sphere for the form the capitalist state would take. Again, the outcome seems almost preordained: The corporate sector would win economic dominance by World War I, though it would not succeed in shaping the state in its image until World War II. Let us briefly review that history.[14]

The drive of business since the beginning of market society has been to dampen competition, mainly through cooperative efforts to limit production and set prices. Before the industrial revolution, the economy of the United States comprised a complex mixture of local and regional markets. Within these markets, leading enterprises customarily attempted to make arrangements to ease competition—most often, price and marketing agreements designed to provide the major firms within each region and industry with a relatively stable guaranteed rate of return. The combined impact of the industrial revolution, massive population increases, the appearance of the rail-road and the telegraph line, and the rapid development of markets in the West destroyed these localized markets and local anticompetitive agreements.

These breathtaking changes in the late nineteenth century had the paradoxical effect of substantially increasing the size of enter-prises while making it more difficult for the largest firms to maintain their market shares and profit levels. Rapidly expanding markets, new technologies, ample investment capital, and easy entry into markets made the environment especially inhospitable to traditional

---

[14] For a summary of the literature on this period, see my *Understanding American Government: The Rise and Decline of the American Political Economy* (New York: John Wiley & Sons, 1979). For more specialized treatments, see Samuel P. Hays, *The Response to Industrialization: 1885-1914* (Chicago: University of Chicago Press, 1957); Gabriel Kolko, *The Triumph of Conservatism: A Reinterpretation of American History, 1900-1916* (Chicago: Quadrangle Books, 1967); Robert H. Wiebe, *The Search for Order: 1879-1920* (New York: Hill & Wang, 1967); Paul Conkin, *The New Deal* (New York: Crowell, 1967); Broadus Mitchell, *Depression Decade* (New York: Holt, 1947); and Gabriel Kolko, *Main Currents in American History* (New York: Harper & Row, 1976).

anticompetitive arrangements. Major firms therefore abandoned tacit anticompetitive agreements to protect their market shares in favor of more formal arrangements, including buying and selling pools, price regulation associations, syndicates, and, when these proved too easily broken, the trust and the holding company. The final step in the process of dampening competition was for competing companies to merge, which was made possible by the states of New Jersey and Delaware in the 1890s. Each introduced liberal incorporation laws under which a corporation could buy stock of a competing enterprise and merge with it into a single legal and economic entity. So momentous were these combined economic, legal, and organizational developments that in the relatively short time between the end of the Civil War and the beginning of World War I, the economy of the United States changed from one of farms and small businesses to one dominated by a handful of industrial and financial corporations.

The incorporated form of business thus culminated decades of efforts by large businesses to form cooperative arrangements aimed at limiting production, apportioning markets, and setting prices. Ultimately, however, these tactics proved inadequate to protect the major firms in each industry from intense competition, falling prices, and declining profits. Some of the most far-sighted business leaders in the corporate sector came to realize that what would help build the most formidable and lasting cartel-like intercorporate understandings would be the sponsorship of the federal government. Government support would legitimate intercorporate cooperation as being in the public interest; it would put new competitors at a disadvantage; and it would protect corporate prerogatives from the hostile inroads of state legislatures.

In the opening years of the twentieth century, then, with the encouragement of some of the leaders of the nation's largest corporations and financial institutions, a new corporate movement began. Its proponents lauded the economic and social benefits of concentrated corporate size and business cooperation—efficiency, economies of scale, technological advance, peaceful industrial relations, and the like—and urged that the federal government support and nurture this new "cooperative capitalism." Out of this movement, in a history too complex to review here, came such legal and political landmarks as the Federal Trade Commission Act, the Federal Reserve System, the War Industries Board of World War I, the trade association movement of the 1920s, the National Industrial Recovery Act and Wagner Labor Relations Act of Roosevelt's New Deal, and a host of other regulatory and subsidy programs, whose overall effect was to "quasi-cartelize" the American economy under federal government sponsorship.

From the early years of the twentieth century, then, the leaders of the largest corporations realized that a stable, ordered economy was possible only with the cooperative intervention of government. This was a view that was not initially shared by all leaders of large enterprises, though it gradually won over those who counted in the corporate sector. What eventually evolved was a protective umbrella of public policy under which the dominant corporations could legally cooperate with each other, stabilize and regularize their relationships in trade associations, standardize practices and products within industries, and receive assistance and subsidies from the government when the situation required. This structure has been the core of the American political economy ever since.

These developments point to a deep fissure within industrial capitalism which appeared in the first decades of the twentieth century and has reappeared intermittently ever since. On one side is a competitive sector of small and medium-sized businesses; on the other, a corporate sector of concentrated, interlocked, and cooperating enterprises which—not without conflict and backsliding within its own ranks, to be sure—continually turns to the federal government for protection and for coordination of national economic activities. Although they are united on some of the basics (the rights of property, the sanctity of contracts), these two fractions of capitalism have remained divided over what functions are appropriate for the capitalist state. This conflict can be seen in virtually every area of public policy related to business, but nowhere more dramatically than in the two groups' opposed approaches to the issue of labor organization.

Small and medium-sized businesses, because their situation is so competitive, have always been hostile to unionization and collective bargaining. The corporations have taken a different view, however. As early as the turn of the century, far-sighted leaders of major enterprises recognized that a stable economic environment conducive to corporate growth and profitability was impossible without a peaceful, cooperative labor force. A small but influential wing of the corporate fraction was firmly committed to cooperative rather than competitive capitalism. From at least 1900 onward, influential business leaders and a handful of business organizations advocated collective bargaining to regularize labor contracts, eliminate wildcat strikes, and imbue union leaders with a sense of responsibility for industrial peace.

Years of educational effort by the corporately founded and

financed National Civic Federation and the American Association of Labor Legislation helped make collective-bargaining agreements widespread in the railroad industry by the beginning of World War I. The powerful War Industries Board that directed the American economy during the war years, composed mainly of representatives of the great corporations and banks, strongly encouraged collective bargaining by bartering government authorization of cartel-like business arrangements for industry agreement to allow employees to form labor organizations. Testimony from some of the major business and labor leaders of the period suggests that this wartime experience in cooperative capitalism provided a powerful precedent and model for later developments in collective bargaining. That experience convinced not only labor leaders such as Samuel Gompers and Sidney Hillman of the attractiveness of business-union collaboration, but also business and political leaders such as Bernard Baruch, Gerard Swope, Herbert Hoover, and Franklin Roosevelt as well.

This sympathy toward labor-management cooperation as a means of stabilizing the corporate environment had its most important expression in Section 7(a) of the National Industrial Recovery Act, passed in the first hectic days of Roosevelt's New Deal. Section 7(a) guaranteed the right of employees to organize and to bargain collectively. Interestingly, 7(a) was not advocated by a single labor-union leader. Rather, it was the culmination of the efforts of those business leaders who envisioned a cooperative, regulated capitalism in which the great corporations were guaranteed a predictable and stable environment by unionization, national collective bargaining contracts, and state regulation of the economy.[15]

In the crisis of the Great Depression, the leaders of the New Deal accepted the analysis long advocated by the most progressive elements of the corporate fraction, that the way out of economic crisis was down the road of cooperative capitalism. The right of working people to bargain collectively was an integral part of that analysis. To be sure, this view was not shared by most businessmen in the United States, which accounts for some of the bitterness of labor-management relations during the Depression. Indeed, most businesspeople remained openly hostile to labor organizations during the 1930s, as was starkly demonstrated by the widespread antilabor violence during that period. Influential leaders in the business class, however, closely tied to the most powerful corporations and financial

[15] The Wagner Act, the law that serves as the basis for modern forms of collective bargaining, was in many ways merely a response to the turmoil unleased by 7(a). The act put in place the machinery necessary to enforce the provisions of 7(a).

institutions, saw collective bargaining as the necessary centerpiece of industrial peace—and saw their aspirations transformed into federal law. In time, the corporate fraction would enjoy a federally sponsored and regulated structure for regularizing cooperative relations between the major corporations and labor unions. That structure of law and services helped to ensure that most bargaining between workers and management would take place through their respective attorneys, not through confrontation at the workplace.

By the end of the Second World War, the transformation of public policy was virtually complete, and the modern capitalist state was a reality. As yet, not all the machinery of regulation, subsidization, business-cycle management, militarization of the economy, welfare control of the underclass, collective bargaining, and protection of overseas business operations was in finished form. Still, the capitalist state as an institution committed to the support, protection, and sustenance of the major corporate enterprises was widely accepted by business, political, and academic leaders. Formally transforming the Constitution so as to change the definition of the state from an institution supportive of laissez-faire capitalism to one more attuned to concentrated corporate capitalism would naturally be a longer and more tortuous process than altering public policy, but the end would be the same.

Before 1900, when the corporations had not yet emerged as the dominant capitalist fraction, the Supreme Court functioned primarily as an instrument of the dominant class in general and not as an instrument of intraclass division. In the second half of the nineteenth century, the Supreme Court became the virtual handmaiden of private property. During that period, the Court rendered a series of decisions that reaffirmed the status of corporations as persons and holders of rights, and therefore as entities to be left free from interference in their operations. The Court interpreted the due process clause of the Fourteenth Amendment, originally intended to protect newly enfranchised black citizens, as a prohibition against state regulation of business enterprises and against efforts by working people to form unions. The Court also interpreted the Sherman Antitrust Act, originally directed at the problem of business monopoly, as prohibiting the unionization of workers.

For most of its history, in fact, from the era of John Marshall through the 1920s, the Court substantially agreed with the interests and needs of the leading national economic institutions. In the last decades of this era, in particular, the Court actively protected corporations from the dual threat of regulation by state governments and a unionized work force. This happy relationship was torn asunder by the events that surrounded the collapse of American capitalism in 1929. The crisis of capitalism was reflected in a crisis of the Court. In response to the Great Depression, the most advanced sectors of the business community and national political leadership moved in directions sharply at odds with prevailing notions on the Court. While members of the Court remained tied to fairly strict laissez-faire notions, corporate and political leaders were becoming sensitive to the necessity of constructing a form of cooperative corporate capitalism in which the national government would be actively involved in the protection, coordination, and stabilization of the entire economy. When the Roosevelt administration moved actively to implement this idea with legislation, the Court responded by rejecting many of the landmark programs of the New Deal, the most important ones being minimum-wage legislation, the National Industrial Recovery Act, and the Agricultural Adjustment Act.

Nevertheless, the constitutional crisis was short-lived. For reasons that are unclear, and without any change in personnel, the Court began to find New Deal legislation perfectly acceptable after 1937, including the new conception of governmental activism. Whether this transformation was influenced most centrally by the power of public opinion as reflected in FDR's smashing 1936 electoral victory, by the fear elicited among the justices by Roosevelt's ill-fated plan to pack the Court with friendly jurists, or by pressures from corporate and financial leaders, is largely immaterial. What mattered was that after 1937, the Court returned to the fold. From then until the present, the Court has allowed the federal government virtually a free hand in regulating and coordinating corporate capitalism.

The Present. Since about the early 1950s, American capitalism has enjoyed an interval of steady economic growth and consensus on political fundamentals among the elite. Now, however, I believe we are entering a new period of intracapitalist struggle over the nature of the state. That struggle will probably center on how much the state should intervene in market relations, with one side articulating a vision of government-corporate planning and the other a return to a more pristine laissez-faire policy. What is striking about this emerging debate is its slightly faded character, its recycled arguments and proposals reminiscent of earlier periods of intracapitalist struggle. There is, however, a critical difference. In both the intracapitalist struggles of the past, the fight was between fractions representing a declining form of capitalism and an emergent and dynamic one. Now, however, the struggle seems to be between a fraction articulating a vision of the state appropriate to a capitalism that began its decline a century ago (the laissez-faire form) and a fraction articulating a vision appropriate to a capitalism that is presently in disarray (the government-corporate planning form). This seeming poverty of intracapitalist debate, coupled with the intensity and bad temper that accompanies it, points to the profundity of the present crisis.

The broad outlines of the crisis are now coming into focus. Most important, it is now evident that the pillars of American economic, political, military, and ideological supremacy since World War II are all crumbling to one degree or another. America's position of strength, economic advance, and stable social relations since World War II has been based on a unique confluence of factors. First, the ravages of two world wars left America's principal capitalist rivals prostrate and dependent upon U.S. economic, financial, and military resources, as well as helpless to prevent American economic penetration into their former colonies and privileged economic zones. America emerged from the war as the dominant capitalist nation, as well as the leading imperialist power, with all the attendant privileges of surplus extraction. Second, the United States came out of the war with the most powerful and productive industrial system the world had ever seen; and for a time the nation was able to provide its citizens with an unmatched and steadily advancing standard of living. This industrial machine was fueled, of course, by the boost given its productive and technological infrastructure by the war, as well as by the militarization of the American economy under the cold war. Finally, Keynesian theory contributed to the stability of mature capitalism by interpreting the experiences of the Great Depression and war mobilization in a way that encouraged government to formulate policies and create tools for the management of the economy as a whole. For a time, the resulting arrangements safely contained the contradictions inherent in capitalism.

Each of these advantages has since deteriorated or disintegrated. Unchallenged American hegemony in the world capitalist system has given way to renewed economic rivalry among the leading capitalist nations and a revolt by important sections of the formerly dependent third world. These changes in turn have ended the exclusive access American goods formerly had to overseas markets and escalated the prices of raw materials. The United States thus can no longer depend on its world position to protect the health and vitality of its home front, to provide the breathing space it needs to work out the contradictions in its own economy. The transformations in the world capitalist economy also have exacerbated the problems of inflation, unemployment, fiscal deterioration, and multiple externalities such as pollution, waste of resources, and disruption of society, which modern capitalism generates as a matter of course. Taken together, these developments, in my view, signal the end of the era of capitalist accumulation, expansion, and prosperity and the beginning of an era of contraction and declining living standards.

Finally, in the face of mounting troubles, the traditional Keynesian tools of economic management have proved decreasingly effective. Yet, alarmingly, no new tools seem to be available that offer even a vague promise of rationally managing the system. We are now in the uncomfortable position of being unable to discard our present set of managerial tools; we cannot afford to keep on using them, but we have no new steering strategies to replace them.

One additional development has contributed to the present environment of decline; namely, what might be called a legitimation crisis, a developing sense at all levels that the present political system is incapable of meeting the challenges that face us as a people. It is certainly no secret that the confidence of the American people in the primary institutions of our society and its leaders is at a historic ebb, with no sign that this discontent is a passing phenomenon. Whether opinion polls ask about confidence in political and business leaders, doctors, or teachers, about the justice and efficacy of the political or economic system, or about people's present situation or faith in the future, respondents almost invariably answer negatively. Involvement and participation in the political life of the country are also at a historic nadir. Discontent, cynicism, and malaise seem to grip the vast majority of citizens in the United States.

Crisis usually causes elite groups to start a desperate search for solutions. In the present crisis facing the American system, intra-capitalist debate over what new direction public policy should take has involved two principal points of view. The first emphasizes the need to reinvigorate the market mechanism by radically reducing the activity of the federal government in business regulation, economic management, and welfare activities. This return to a nineteenth-century laissez-faire attitude toward the political economy can be seen in the Reaganite capture of the Republican party, the grip of the conservatives on the Democratic party through Jimmy Carter, the visibility and popularity of Friedman-style economic theory, the sales figures of books written by such authors as William Simon, Howard Jarvis, and Robert Ringer, the persistent grumbling in all walks of life about government interference, and a variety of other indicators too numerous to detail.

Nevertheless, I cannot see how this point of view can sustain itself as a policy line in the long run. For one thing, it ignores the entire history of the development of the modern capitalist state—particularly that state's emergence as a product both of popular revulsion at the effects of the untrammeled free market and of corporate efforts to create a stable, predictable economic environment. The laissez-faire view also overlooks the political power of the concentrated corporate sector which helped to create and continues to benefit from current arrangements. It seems to me, then, that the laissez-faire tendency within the dominant class, while temporarily ascendant, cannot long endure, though I have no doubt that this view will continue to be fervently articulated as long as capitalism exists in the United States.

The principal competing viewpoint within the capitalist class favors what I would call corporate-oriented national planning. This position is temporarily in eclipse; but I suspect it will prove to be the more enduring. Although the idea of planning brings tremors to many, it seems likely to be the destiny of capitalist market economies. The problems endemic to industrial market capitalism—stagnation, inflation, resource shortages, community disruptions, and pollution—are now so huge, complex, and interrelated that simply to turn them over to the free market, simply to allow the economy to run its course without direction, would be madness. Unplanned market capitalism cannot help capriciously using up its essential resources and drowning in its own effluent, not to mention experiencing severe economic shocks and the social disruptions attached to them. Planning of some sort may be the only possible solution. As economic philosopher Robert Heilbroner has put it:

> The general prognosis for the immediate future seems very clear. The next phase of capitalism must be an increasingly planned system. . . . What conservatives fail to see is that there is no alternative to planning if capitalism is to be kept alive at all.[16]

Even in the midst of the present free-enterprise celebration, the demand for forms of limited, sectorial planning can be heard from diverse quarters. Many Americans, for instance, want to see government plans for energy development and use, transportation, housing,

[16] Robert L. Heilbroner, *Business Civilization in Decline* (New York: W. W. Norton & Company, 1976), p. 34.

and health care. Despite antigovernment talk, people tend to turn to government when a set of problems begins to spin out of control. Bit by bit, problem by problem, government has increased and inevitably will continue to increase its involvements and its machinery for intervention. As powerful institutions and people demand that these bits and pieces of trouble-shooting machinery be used in more coherent and rational ways, the road to planning is opened irrevocably. As Andrew Shonfield has pointed out, "To adopt a principle of economic nonintervention by the state is at least intelligible; what does not make sense is to intervene constantly and yet not to plan."[17] At this point, the call for planning in the United States is being heard not only from the traditional social-democratic Left, but from the very pinnacle of the economic system. Limited economic planning is now part of the program of groups like the Trilateral Commission and the Business Advisory Council and part of the appeals of influential economic leaders such as bankers David Rockefeller and Felix Rohatyn. The prerequisites of planning, furthermore—sophisticated economic forecasting and reliable economic indicators, as well as the rhetorical commitment by government to full employment, controlled inflation, and rational use of resources—are all solidly in place.

The Future. Capitalist planning, it hardly need be added, surely will not be of the variety so dear to the hearts of socialists. Given the present distribution of economic and political power in the United States, I have no doubt that should planning arrive, it will be by and for the major corporations. Planning will be directed toward enhancing the position, profitability, and stability of the major corporations behind an elaborate rhetorical facade celebrating universal benefits. Heilbroner poses the issues dramatically:

> Governments, for all their ideological skirmishes with business, have always been the silent partners of business; indeed, as Adam Smith was explicit in declaring, private property would not exist a "single night" without government. . . . The drift of business society will be toward a business-government state.[18]

Planning will represent, then, an additional weapon for the protection of power and privilege.

[17] Andrew Shonfield, *Modern Capitalism* (London: Oxford University Press, 1965), p. 297.
[18] Heilbroner, *Business Civilization in Decline*, pp. 34, 93.

We are still in the opening years of what I perceive to be a new period of troubles and of intracapitalist struggle, so it is premature to make predictions about the character of the emerging capitalist state and its constitutional system.[19] All we can observe about the future with any confidence are the broad outlines of emerging tendencies toward crisis and the competing policy options addressed to them. As always, with respect to the future, we are left mostly with questions, not answers. Let me raise for consideration what I consider to be several of the most compelling.

So far, the new era has produced two general policy tendencies, the laissez-faire and the corporate-planning positions. Are additional approaches likely to emerge in the face of mounting troubles? At the moment, given the traditionally narrow boundaries of political debate in the United States, it is difficult to see where other tendencies might come from. It does not seem likely, at least in the short run, that any will appear from outside the boundaries of the capitalist class. A moribund Left, in particular, seems incapable of breaking into the American political arena. Nor are there indications within the capitalist class of other emergent tendencies, at least if one looks at the business press, the positions of political parties, or the formulations of business leaders. The laissez-faire and corporate-planning tendencies have the virtue (and perhaps the disadvantage) of being familiar and comfortable, the one a throwback to an earlier stage in American history, the other a linear advance (in giant steps, to be sure) of developments in the capitalist state for most of the twentieth century. If either should prove equal to some of the problems we face, I see no reason why capitalist fractions would stray far afield for another alternative.

It is still too early to know which of the competing tendencies (assuming there remain only two general ones) will win out in the end, which one will eventually impose its vision on the form, operations, and purposes of the state. My guess, as I have suggested, is that corporate-oriented planning is the likely future of American capitalism. Still, the powerful appeal of laissez-faire may yet upset my expectations. We have no way of predicting, moreover, whether either conception of the capitalist state is capable of successfully taming the emerging crises in the system. In my view, neither seems up to the task, the one having proved already that it was not equal to the problems generated by a far simpler capitalist economy and the other being in some respects merely a further development of public

[19] There will doubtless be increasingly severe interclass struggles as well, though their consideration is beyond the scope of this discussion.

policies that have contributed significantly to our present difficulties. I may be underestimating their flexibility, innovative potential, and staying power, however. Finally, because it is too early to know which policy will prevail, it is impossible to say what the future capitalist state and its supporting constitutional system will look like. My preliminary guess, based on some of the theoretical work already coming from the corporate-planning fraction[20] and on technical developments in information gathering, storing, and analysis, is that it will prove to be a more authoritarian system.[21]

One final observation about this new period is in order. The debate between the two main policy positions has been evident primarily within the capitalist class; it has not yet moved onto the terrain of public discourse. Indeed, debate in the political arena at present seems strangely divorced from that within the capitalist class, being confined mainly to the relative virtues of limited government and the free market versus New Deal–style liberalism. Yet it seems to me likely that planning is the probable capitalist future. If that is so, then the present shape of public discourse in the United States is diversionary and beside the point. If we as a people are not to drift unconsciously into corporate-dominated planning, we must begin to raise questions about the kind of planning system most appropriate to a democratic system. If we fail to do so, the issues will be settled for us.

[20] See especially Michael Crozier et al., eds., *The Crisis of Democracy* (New York: New York University Press, 1975).
[21] For a chilling discussion of these tendencies see Bertram Gross, *Friendly Fascism* (New York: Evans, 1980).

3

The Constitution and Hamiltonian Capitalism

Forrest McDonald

If one were to take a poll of American historians and ask what sort of economic system was contemplated by the framers of the Constitution, the most common answer would doubtless be capitalism. That answer is inaccurate, but it is understandable. The misconception arises partly from the way things turned out after the adoption of the Constitution, but more basically from the fact that eighteenth-century Americans clearly regarded property rights as sacrosanct and the protection of those rights as a primary end of government. John Locke, whose views were known to virtually every American of the founding generation, had taught that the ownership of property was a natural right, antecedent to civil society; and the state constitutions and bills of rights adopted during the Revolutionary era gave ringing approval to that dictum. James Madison, speaking at the Constitutional Convention in 1787, cited "the security of property" first among "the primary objects of civil society," and most of the other delegates shared that view. Friends of the proposed Constitution insisted that increased security for property would be among the main advantages of ratification. Anti-Federalists, seeking even more protection, brought about the Fifth Amendment's explicit declaration that "no person shall . . . be deprived of . . . property, without due process of law; nor shall private property be taken for public use without just compensation."[1]

The emergence of capitalism, however, required a good deal more than legal recognition of private property rights. Private property existed under feudalism, after all; indeed, in the economic sense,

[1] Max Farrand, ed., *The Records of the Federal Convention of 1787*, 4 vols. (New Haven, Conn.: Yale University Press, 1937), vol. 1, p. 147; Forrest McDonald, "Historical Origins of the Taking Clause of the Fifth Amendment," in Stanley Katz, ed., *Nor Shall Property Be Taken* (forthcoming).

feudalism can be defined as a system of inherited property relationships, protecting equally the (unequal) private rights of all. For property to be capital it must be employed as capital, which is to say used for the purpose of creating more property. I own, for instance, a pickup truck and seventeen acres of land, and while both are property, neither is capital. If I were to use the truck for commercial transportation of goods or people, and subdivide the land for a housing development—both of which I could do if I wished—both would be capital. My ability to put my property to such uses depends on a large number of economic, social, legal, technological, and institutional conditions and circumstances. My unwillingness to do so is largely a function of a system of values and attitudes.

Similarly, for capitalism to come into being, certain conditions, institutions, values, and circumstances were necessary. For reasons I shall try to make clear as I go along, five sets of conditions in particular were indispensable. The first was a set of attitudes toward property: that it be freely transferable from one owner to another, that there be no no discrimination against commercial property rights in favor of the traditional rights of landholders, and that active development of property be socially preferred to passive enjoyment of the rights of ownership. In addition, capitalism depended on at least four more conditions: a general commitment to the proposition that economic growth is both possible and desirable; government approval of private endeavor as the principal instrument of such growth; institutional recognition of the market as the prime—or at least the ideal—determinant of economic value; and legal and institutional means of converting credit into money and capital.

These conditions were only beginning to exist in the 1780s, when the Constitution was adopted. That period was one of transition from ancient zero-sum conceptions of economic activity to modern growth-oriented conceptions. Precapitalistic and anticapitalistic values, attitudes, and institutions, rooted in the feudal past, were far from dead in America, and those of mercantilism—a system in which economic activity was regulated by the state as a means of aggrandizing the international power and prestige of the state—were in full bloom. The new values, looking to free trade, entrepreneurship, and a market economy, were, with few exceptions, little more than a gleam in the eyes of a few advanced thinkers. The establishment of the Constitution thus was a benchmark in the evolution of systems of political economy, for it made possible—though not inevitable—the transformation from the old order to the new.

The Preconditions of Capitalism

Before analyzing the work of the framers of the Constitution, it will be useful to consider the extent to which the five preconditions of capitalism existed in the United States before 1787.

Although it is clear that Americans regarded "private property rights" as sacred, it is not so clear what they meant by the term. Most would doubtless have approved Blackstone's celebrated definition, "that sole and despotic dominion which one man claims and exercises over the external things of the world, in total exclusion of the right of any other individual in the universe."[2] Neither in law nor in practice, however, was the matter so simple as that. The right to property is not *a* right but a complex and subtle combination of many rights, powers, and duties, distributed among individuals, society, and the state. Blackstone, after defining property rights on the second page of his Book II, *Of the Rights of Things,* devoted the remaining 518 pages to qualifying and specifying exceptions to his definition.

Americans, like Englishmen, recognized that, as a condition of their right to acquire and hold private property, their dominion over it was subject to many other rights reserved by the public. As an aggregate of individuals, the public retained (to a lesser or greater extent, varying with time and jurisdiction) rights to grazing, wood gathering, hunting, passage, and water use on privately owned lands. In its corporate or governmental capacity, the public reserved the right to restrict the use of privately owned property and also the right to take it from the owners under certain circumstances. Government's means of taking private property, in addition to regulation, taxation, and eminent domain, included a variety of legal devices inherited from the Middle Ages. (Lest it be supposed that the use of such devices was uncommon in America, it should be recognized that during the Revolutionary War the state governments deprived owners of nearly $100 million of property by one means or another, with neither just compensation nor due process. That sum was close to half the value of all real property in the country.[3])

Moreover, American attitudes and institutions concerning property were biased against capitalism in two crucial ways. One was that personal property in most of its forms was treated as inferior to real property—that is, land. The negotiability of personal notes,

[2] William Blackstone, *Commentaries on the Laws of England, in Four Books,* 12th ed., 4 vols. (London, 1793), vol. 2, p. 2.
[3] McDonald, "Origins of the Taking Clause."

for instance, was not fully recognized in the law. If a note obliging party A to pay a certain sum to party B were transferred to party C, it could cease to be legally enforceable. Insurance law was virtually nonexistent; laws against usury, narrowly defined, obtained in every state. These conditions were not mere matters of oversight, to be rectified routinely in the course of time and progress. Instead, they were reflections of deep-seated popular hostility and suspicion of all forms of "paper" property, including money and stock. Americans had absorbed this attitude from the propaganda of Henry St. John, First Viscount Bolingbroke, and other English Oppositionists, who exalted the virtues of land ownership and deplored the infusion of money into social relationships—a development that was implicit in the Financial Revolution that had transformed England between the 1690s and the 1750s. The ideology of agrarianism would lose its hold slowly in America, and it would never entirely disappear.[4]

The other bias was that land law itself was tilted against development. The assumption underlying the law, as Morton Horwitz has pointed out, "was that land was not essentially an instrumental good or a productive asset but rather a private estate to be enjoyed for its own sake."[5] In his seminal work on the modernization of American law, Horwitz cites numerous ways the common law, as interpreted by American courts in the eighteenth century, discouraged, prevented, or punished efforts by landowners to develop their property and turn it to productive nonagricultural use.

That brings us to the second prerequisite for the emergence of capitalism, a general belief in the desirability and possibility of economic growth. On this subject Americans were of two minds. The mania for "projects" which had swept Britain early in the eighteenth century had infected America by the 1780s. The spread of information on "scientific farming," the chartering of companies to improve navigation on major rivers, the awarding of public and private prizes for useful inventions, the newspapers' enthusiasm for every manner of innovation, and the proliferation of manufacturing schemes in New England all attest to the contagiousness of the spirit of the Age of Improvements. And yet, as Alexander Hamilton's survey of the economy in 1791 made abundantly evident, the number of persons actually engaged in any developmental activity in America was minus-

[4] Morton J. Horwitz, *The Transformation of American Law, 1790-1860* (Cambridge: Harvard University Press, 1977); Isaac Kramnick, *Bolingbroke and His Circle* (Cambridge: Harvard University Press, 1968); Rodger D. Parker, "The Gospel of Opposition: A Study in Eighteenth-Century Anglo-American Ideology" (Ph.D. dissertation, Wayne State University, 1975).

[5] Horwitz, *Transformation of American Law*, p. 36.

cule. South and west of Philadelphia, except for the chartering of a few canal companies and the experiments of a handful of gentlemen farmers, the spirit of improvement was simply not in evidence. In that vast area, as Hamilton and many other observers pointed out, the people were characterized by "constitutional indolence." In New England, much of the energy being put into economic projects was really exploitative rather than developmental—for instance, stripping the coastal forests of ship timber in search of quick profits, with no regard for the future—and was therefore destructive of capital instead of capital-accumulative.[6]

What is more, the very idea of economic growth, with its attendant dangers of luxury and economic inequality, was incompatible with republican principles of political theory, at least in some versions of that theory. Plato, believing that relative equality of property was necessary in a republic, wanted to limit inheritances. Lycurgus, "in the most perfect model of government that was ever framed," that of Sparta, banished trade entirely. Montesquieu, whom Americans read as the latest word on republicanism, taught that it could be sustained only by virtue, meaning "love of the republic"; frugality, simplicity, and a "mediocrity" of "abilities and fortunes" were necessary to sustain that virtue. Indeed, Montesquieu said that if equality broke down, "the republic will be utterly undone," and thus it was "absolutely necessary there should be some regulation in respect to . . . all . . . forms of contracting. For were we once allowed to dispose of our property to whom and how we pleased, the will of each individual would disturb the order of the fundamental law."[7]

Just as important, development was handicapped by the widespread belief that economic growth was not really possible. Most Americans conceived of economic life as John Adams did—as a zero-sum game in which the world's supply of wealth was essentially fixed. One man or one nation might obtain a larger share of that

[6] Treasury Department Circulars, June 22, August 13, 1781, Harold C. Syrett, ed., *The Papers of Alexander Hamilton*, 26 vols. (New York: Columbia University Press, 1961-1979), vol. 8, pp. 497-498; vol. 9, pp. 35-37, and the responses thereto, ibid., vol. 9; Benjamin Lincoln to Hamilton, April 7, 1791, ibid., vol. 8, pp. 248-251. For examples of the spirit of improvement and its limited effects, see New London *Connecticut Gazette*, January 2, 30, February 13, 1784, April 6, 1787; *New York Daily Advertiser*, March 31, 1788; *Providence Gazette and Country Journal*, May 24, 1788; *Newport Mercury*, March 1, 1790.

[7] Montesquieu, *The Spirit of the Laws*, trans. Thomas Nugent (New York: Hafner Publishing Company, 1949), bk. 5, sects. 1-5, pp. 40-46; bk. 7, sect. 1, p. 94; J. G. A. Pocock, *The Machiavellian Moment: Florentine Political Thought and the Atlantic Republican Tradition* (Princeton, N.J.: Princeton University Press, 1975), pp. 387-390, 443, 534, and passim.

wealth, but only at the expense of another man or nation. Even the expansion of the population and the settlement of the American frontier were commonly reckoned in zero-sum terms: If the United States gained people and an accompanying increase of land values, it was through Europe's loss of emigrants and resulting decline in land values. One small group of Americans, which included such Virginia planters as Thomas Jefferson and John Taylor of Caroline, did subscribe to the theories of the French physiocrats, who held that economic growth was possible—but only through work on the land, which they regarded as the sole real source of wealth. When coupled with the prevailing Bolingbrokean ideology, physiocratic theory became not merely precapitalistic but decidedly anticapitalistic. To the physiocrats and their American followers, commercial and manufacturing activity added nothing to the value of things grown or extracted from the earth; while in the Bolingbrokean view, profits from or interest on bank notes, public debt, or corporate stocks were stolen from their true producers and rightful owners, those who labor in the earth.[8]

Such attitudes made a shambles of the third prerequisite of capitalism, state sanction for private developmental activity. For one thing, the prejudice against paper wealth, together with a prejudice against "privileged" wealth in the form of corporate charters, all but precluded the emergence of commercial banking. Of the three banks in the United States, only the Bank of Massachusetts had been able to obtain and retain a charter. The Bank of New York had tried in vain to get a charter in 1783, then took the risk of operating without one; Philadelphia's Bank of North America had obtained a charter from Pennsylvania in 1782, only to see the fickle state legislature revoke it in 1785.[9]

State governments did more, however, than simply impede private developmental activities. In the spirit of mercantilism, they regarded such activity—to the extent that it was legitimate at all—as being properly promoted by government, not by unimpeded private

---

[8] Leslie Wharton, "Conflicting Theories of Republican Economy in the New Nation" (Ph.D. dissertation, Princeton, 1979); Drew R. McCoy, *The Elusive Republic* (Chapel Hill: University of North Carolina Press, 1980); Zoltan Haraszti, *John Adams and the Prophets of Progress* (Cambridge: Harvard University Press, 1952); John Taylor, *A Definition of Parties; or The Political Effects of the Paper System Considered* (Philadelphia, 1794), and *An Enquiry into the Principles and Policy of the Government of the United States* (Fredericksburg, Va., 1814).

[9] Bray Hammond, *Banks and Politics in America from the Revolution to the Civil War* (Princeton, N.J.: Princeton University Press, 1957).

enterprise. Every state legislature enacted a mercantilist system after independence, to a lesser or greater extent. The government of North Carolina attempted to go into business as a marketer of the state's tobacco crop, with rather comically disastrous results. New York's government, under the leadership of Governor George Clinton, initiated and started carrying out a wide range of developmental projects; New York became a pioneer in using the mixed corporation, owned partly by government and partly by private investors, as an instrument of economic development.[10]

The fourth prerequisite, allowing the market to set economic value, existed only to a limited extent in America. It is true that the prices of most goods moving in international, interstate, and even intrastate commerce were free to respond to fluctuations in demand. Moreover, in America as nowhere in Europe, most land could be bought and sold as a commodity at whatever price the market would support. But the price of bread was set by assize in most American cities; rates charged by millers, ferrymen, draymen, keepers of inns and taverns, and operators of other "public utilities" were fixed by law. Marketing practices were regulated by the common law and by statute; mercantilist codes required inspection of many goods and prohibited, taxed, or gave bounties to the movement of others; and the allowable interest on loans was fixed by usury laws. What is more, legislatures felt free to interfere in buying, selling, and lending even after deals had been transacted. During the war, for instance, Virginia planters were enabled to write off debts to British merchants amounting to £273,554 (about $1.2 million) by taking advantage of the state's misnamed Sequestration Act. South Carolina planters, after importing lavishly at war's end and subsequently finding themselves unable to pay for what they had bought, cavalierly passed laws staying executions on their debts. Other states enacted similar legislation. Patrick Henry expressed a common American disdain for the free operation of the market when he declared that "there are thousands

[10] The generalization about state mercantilistic systems is based upon my study of the legislative journals and session laws of each of the states; see, for example, the messages of Governor James Bowdoin to the Massachusetts legislature, May 31, June 2, 1785, February 8, 21, 1786, in the manuscript journal of the House of Representatives, Massachusetts Archives, and in the published *Acts and Laws of the Commonwealth of Massachusetts*, 13 vols. (Boston, 1781-1789, by session). Regarding the North Carolina episode, see James Iredell and François X. Martin, eds., *The Public Acts of the General Assembly of North Carolina*, 2 vols. (New Bern, N.C., 1804), vol. 1, pp. 393-395, and Merrill Jensen, *The New Nation* (New York: Alfred A. Knopf, 1950), pp. 319-320. Regarding Clinton and New York, see Alfred F. Young, *The Democratic Republicans of New York: The Origins, 1763-1797* (Chapel Hill: University of North Carolina Press, 1967).

and thousands of contracts, whereof equity forbids an exact literal performance."[11]

Underlying arbitrary government interference in the market was an archaic concept of the contract, one based on the medieval idea of the inherent justice or fairness of an exchange, which in turn rested on the notion that everything had, intrinsically, a fair value and therefore a just price. In England, by the 1780s, a modern market definition of the obligations of contract had evolved: "It is the consent of parties alone that fixes the just price of any thing, without reference to the nature of things themselves, or to their intrinsic value." That construction of the nature of contracts had not yet been established in any American jurisdiction, however.[12]

The final prerequisite for capitalism is the necessity for institutional means of turning credit into cash or capital. Those means were not only lacking; under existing arrangements, they were prevented from developing. Usury laws, legal restrictions on the negotiability of notes and other instruments of credit, legislative capriciousness in regard to banking and contracts, and perhaps above all the agrarian ideology stood as virtually insurmountable obstacles to the development of a viable credit system. In addition, those whose need for credit was most immediate—the members of the commercial community—had a mental barrier regarding it. Merchants granted credit to planters and country gentlemen against their future crops in the expectation of a high level of default and fraud, and they marked up their prices enough to cover the anticipated losses; but among merchants themselves, credit was personal and a matter of respectability. With good family connections or recommendations, plus a reputation for reliability, integrity, trustworthiness, and ability, a person could get credit even without collateral. Without these hallmarks of respectability, credit was not forthcoming, no matter how much collateral the applicant had to offer. In other words, eighteenth-century merchants had an ingrained skepticism of the kind of depersonalized,

---

[11] Colonial interferences in the market, though not commonly known and not the subject of any systematic treatise, can be confirmed through study of local records and histories. Common law restrictions on marketing practices are summarized in Blackstone, *Commentaries*, vol. 4, pp. 154-159. For the Virginia debt cancellations, see Isaac S. Harrell, *Loyalism in Virginia: Chapters in the Economic History of the Revolution* (Durham, N.C.: Duke University Press, 1926); regarding South Carolina, see the legislative proceedings reported in *Charleston Evening Gazette* beginning September 28, 1785, and Thomas Cooper and Daniel McCord, eds., *Statutes at Large of South Carolina*, 10 vols. (Columbia, S.C., 1836-1840), vol. 4, pp. 710-716. Henry's remark is in Jonathan Elliot, ed., *The Debates in the Several State Conventions on the Adoption of the Federal Constitution*, 5 vols. (Philadelphia: Lippincott, 1861), vol. 3, pp. 318-319.

[12] Horwitz, *Transformation of American Law*, pp. 160ff.

collateral-based credit that is essential to large-scale capitalist enterprise. (Imagine trying to finance General Motors or American Telephone & Telegraph on the basis of the personal reputations of its chief financial officers.)

For all these reasons, Americans had been unable to develop a workable and acceptable system whereby future expectations could be turned into money. Few, indeed, had given the matter any thought, though the materials for creating such a system had been at hand since the war. Those materials were the nation's Revolutionary War debts, as I shall explain later. The know-how for using public debts as the basis of private credit and currency also was readily available—all one needed to do was study the examples of the Netherlands and England. Not many Americans were thinking along those lines, however; and in any event, there was no central government with the taxing power necessary to make an adaptation of the Dutch and English systems work in America. Consequently, the public debt was a public burden, crushing the economic activity of which it could have been the life's blood.

The Intentions behind the Constitution

The merest glance at the Constitution is enough to show that the document did not, in a stroke, terminate existing conditions and usher in the age of capitalism. A somewhat closer look indicates that the Constitution did make the transformation possible. Much more careful scrutiny is necessary if we are to ascertain the extent to which any or all of the Founding Fathers intended that such a transformation should take place.

Broadly speaking, the features of the Constitution that bear on the question at hand—what sort of political economy was contemplated by the framers?—are of two general types. One group comprises specific provisions in the form of requirements imposed on the national and state governments. The other group, which established the general rules governing the levying of taxes and making provision for the public debts, was more open-ended, leaving a large measure of discretion to Congress.

The specific constitutional mandates had anticapitalist as well as procapitalist implications, but on balance they leaned toward the capitalistic world that was aborning. The most important negative feature was that the police power—the power to regulate the health, safety, well-being, and morals of the people—was left in the hands of the states. The police power had traditionally been exercised in ways inimical to entrepreneurship and a free market. Several delegates to the Constitutional Convention, notably James Madison of Virginia and Charles Pinckney of South Carolina, proposed to limit the states' entire triumvirate of reserved powers (police, taxation, and eminent domain) by giving Congress a veto over state legislation, but they failed to win much support. At the opposite extreme, George Mason of Virginia urged that Congress be vested with power to enact sumptuary legislation (laws regulating morality) but found no supporters. That was a victory for free enterprise.[13]

Two other specific features of the Constitution were tilted strongly in favor of a free-market system. The first consisted of the several provisions that made the United States the largest area of free trade—meaning trade unimpeded by internal barriers or other restrictions—in the world. Given the spirit of the times, however, it should not be surprising to learn that even this aspect of the Constitution was viewed by both its friends and its foes in mercantilistic terms. That is to say that Northerners, who owned most American shipping, regarded the creation of a common-market America as a way of excluding Europeans from competition, whereas Southerners, as growers of agricultural staples for international markets, feared just such an exclusion on the ground that it would drive freight rates upward. The South proposed to defend its interests by insisting that the Constitution require a two-thirds majority of both houses of Congress for the passage of acts regulating and taxing trade; but this position was rejected both in the Constitutional Convention and during the subsequent consideration of amendments suggested by the ratifying conventions.[14]

Among the most important provisions are those of Article I, Section 10, which restrict the powers of the states. Some of the prohibitions are political rather than economic ("no State shall enter into any Treaty, Alliance, or Confederation; grant Letters of Marque and Reprisal"). Others, though superficially political or related only to criminal matters ("[no state shall] pass any Bill of Attainder, ex post facto law"), must have been designed at least in part to prevent a repetition of the wartime history of expropriations by state governments.

---

[13] Farrand, *Records*, vol. 1, pp. 164-165; vol. 2, pp. 344, 606; Charles F. Hobson, "The Negative on State Laws: James Madison, the Constitution, and the Crisis of Republican Government," *William and Mary Quarterly*, April 1979, pp. 215-235.

[14] Farrand, *Records*, vol. 2, pp. 183, 190-191, 210-211, 374-375, 449-453; Elliot, *Debates*, vol. 2, pp. 58, 83ff.

Inclusion of the Contract Clause. The central clause in Article I, Section 10, and the one which pointed the United States most directly toward a capitalistic future, is the contract clause: "No State shall . . . pass any . . . Law impairing the Obligation of Contracts." Read broadly, literally, unequivocally, and without regard to the context of the times, the contract clause appears to indicate that the Founding Fathers rejected the existing economic order and endorsed the order that was to come. Such, however, is not the case: The contract clause was shrouded in ambiguity, from its initial proposal to the strange way it was incorporated into the Constitution to the way it was viewed by contemporaries.

The first proposal for a version of the contract clause arose late in the Constitutional Convention. On August 28, the delegates voted to amend the twelfth article of the report of the Committee of Detail to read, "No state shall coin money, nor emit bills of credit, nor make any thing but gold and silver coin a tender in payment of debts." Rufus King of Massachusetts then moved to add, in language taken from the Northwest Ordinance, "a prohibition on the States to interfere in private contracts." In the light of subsequent interpretations of the contract clause, that language is significant: "In the just preservation of rights and property, it is understood and declared, that no law ought ever to be made, or have force in the said territory, that shall, in any manner whatever, interfere with or affect private contracts or engagements, *bona fide*, and without fraud, previously formed."[15]

The response to King's motion was generally negative. Gouverneur Morris of Pennsylvania objected that "this would be going too far." The federal courts would prevent abuses insofar as that was within their jurisdiction, said Morris, but within a state "a majority must rule, whatever may be the mischief done among themselves." George Mason echoed Morris's sentiments. Luther Martin of Maryland, though not recorded as having spoken, later indicated that he too opposed the proposal. James Madison expressed mixed feelings. James Wilson of Pennsylvania supported the motion, but he emphasized that only *retrospective* interferences were to be prohibited. At that point a curious thing happened: John Rutledge of South Carolina offered a substitute motion to prohibit bills of attainder and ex post facto laws—as if that would accomplish the purpose of King's

---

[15] Farrand, *Records*, vol. 2, p. 439. The relevant passage of the Northwest Ordinance is in Henry Steele Commager, ed., *Documents of American History*, 7th ed. (New York: Appleton Century Crofts, 1963), p. 131.

motion. Rutledge's substitute motion was passed, seven states to three.[16]

It is important, in attempting to understand the kind of economic system the framers had in mind, to be clear about what happened on August 28. Neither King's original motion nor Rutledge's far weaker substitute had the broad procapitalistic implications contained in the contract clause that was ultimately adopted. King's use of the words *"bona fide,* and without fraud" would have provided abundant room for preserving the fair-value and just-price theory of contract and would have precluded the Marshall Court's landmark decision in *Fletcher* v. *Peck,* in which a state law repealing a previous legislative grant of land was declared unconstitutional despite demonstrable fraud in the original grant. Its use of the words "private contracts" would have precluded both *Fletcher* v. *Peck* and *Dartmouth College* v. *Woodward,* in which the Supreme Court ruled that a legislature could not alter a corporation's charter, because both cases turned on the interpretation of public grants and corporate charters as contracts. King's contract clause was rejected, however— surely a clear indication that a large majority of the delegates opposed the inclusion of a broad, market-oriented contract clause.

How, then, did the clause find its way into the Constitution? The answer is that the Committee of Style put it there at the last minute. That the committee would presume to include in the finished document features the convention as a whole had either not approved or actually rejected is explicable by two circumstances. First, by the second week of September, when the Committee of Style was appointed and did its work, the delegates were tired, harassed, and in a hurry to finish their work and go home, and they were disinclined to pay meticulous attention to every word of the draft. Second, the delegates had before them no list of what they had agreed to, but only a general record of the proceedings, which made checking on the Committee of Style difficult and tedious. That the committee was frustrated in one attempt to slip something over on the convention— a change in punctuation that would have made the general welfare clause a positive grant of power rather than a limitation on the taxing power—is documented.[17] In any event, it appears that the contract clause was the work of the five members of the Committee of Style rather than the body of the convention.

The mystery does not, however, end there. With no record of the committee's deliberations, it has always been assumed that Gouverneur Morris was right when he claimed, many years afterward,

[16] Farrand, *Records,* vol. 2, pp. 439-440, vol. 3, pp. 214-215.
[17] Ibid., vol. 3, p. 379.

that he had personally written the Constitution, with only minor help from the other four members of the Committee of Style.[18] If that is so, then one might further assume that Morris was the author of the contract clause; certainly he was a man of sufficient audacity to take such a liberty. But Morris had opposed the contract clause when King proposed it, and the grounds of his opposition applied just as well to the clause that emerged from the committee two weeks later.

That leaves, as possible sources of the clause, the remaining four members of the committee: James Madison, William Samuel Johnson of Connecticut, Rufus King, and Alexander Hamilton. There is nothing in the recorded speeches or extant writings of Madison and Johnson to indicate that either of them saw the contract clause as other than a redundancy, a reemphasis of the Constitutional prohibitions against paper money and tender laws; and there is therefore no reason to suppose that either of them would have suggested adding it. King had proposed the original clause, but he had hedged his proposal with restrictions that would greatly have reduced its potency. That leaves Hamilton.

Alexander Hamilton's preconvention career as a lawyer, his subsequent conduct as secretary of the treasury, his reasoning in the great Reports, and his avid participation in the movement to modernize contractual relationships all accord with his advocating that a broad, modern conception of contracts be enshrined in fundamental law. Hamilton knew firsthand the advantages of regarding corporate charters as inviolable contracts, for he had represented stockholders when Pennsylvania revoked the charter of the Bank of North America in 1785. Later, in giving an advisory opinion regarding the Yazoo land purchase, he would formulate the first thoroughly reasoned argument that the contract clause of the Constitution was intended to apply to public grants and charters as well as to private agreements. Hamilton was the only one of the committee members who thought along such lines, except insofar as he could persuade the others. That he could have been quite persuasive is evident: Not only did he have great gifts for argument, but he was a long-time intimate friend of Morris's, he held King almost in a hypnotic spell, and he was on intimate political (though not personal) terms with Madison.[19]

[18] Ibid., pp. 419-420.
[19] Forrest McDonald, *Alexander Hamilton: A Biography* (New York: W. W. Norton & Company, 1979), pp. 80-82, 311-313. Hamilton's opinion in the Yazoo case is published in C. Peter Magrath, *Yazoo, Law and Politics in the New Republic: The Case of Fletcher v. Peck* (Providence, R.I.: Brown University Press, 1966), pp. 149-150. Hamilton would have allowed setting aside some contracts in equity, but none in law. See Federalist No. 80, Syrett, *Hamilton Papers*, vol. 4, p. 671.

There is one other possibility. When the legislature of Pennsylvania chartered the Bank of North America, then repealed the charter, then debated a bill to recharter the bank, the questions whether a corporate charter was a contract and whether the legislature could lawfully repeal an act granting a charter were argued repeatedly. James Wilson, as counsel for the bank (a role he sometimes shared with Gouverneur Morris and in which he was sometimes associated with Hamilton) contended that a charter was in fact a contract and not subject to repeal. Opponents of the bank, who dominated the state's Council of Censors, offered cogent arguments defending the legislature's power to alter or abolish corporate charters; but their arguments collapsed once the contract clause was adopted with the Constitution. Wilson may well have anticipated this, and, though he was not a member of the Committee of Style, may have suggested the clause to Morris or Hamilton or both for that reason.[20]

In any event, it seems certain that the intention of the immediate author (or authors) of the contract clause was compatible with the procapitalistic interpretation later pronounced by the Marshall Court. It seems unlikely that the other delegates at the convention, who approved the clause in almost absent-minded haste, viewed it in that light—or would have accepted it had they so viewed it.

Interpretations of the Contract Clause. As for how the contract clause was understood by Federalist and anti-Federalist propagandists and delegates to the states' ratifying conventions, only two interpretations were suggested, and neither of them was the one Hamilton would later argue. By far the more common view was that the prohibition against legislative impairment of contracts was merely a catch-all extension of the bans on paper money and legal tender laws. As Wilson put it during the Pennsylvania ratifying convention, "There are other ways of avoiding payment of debts," such as "instalment acts, and other acts of a similar effect." Madison treated the clause in a similar, though somewhat broader, light in *The Federalist*, No. 44: He lumped it together with the other restrictions contained in Article 1, Section 10, as designed to stop "the fluctuating policy which has directed the public councils." Madison attributed these "legislative interferences, in cases affecting personal rights," to the handiwork of "enterprising and influential speculators" whose doings profited themselves at the expense of "the more-industrious and less-informed

[20] Philadelphia *Evening Herald*, September 7, 8, 1785, April 1, 1786; Journal of the Council of Censors, August 27, 1784, Public Records Division, Harrisburg, Pa.; James Wilson, *Considerations on the Bank of North America* (Philadelphia, 1785).

part of community." Luther Martin, who opposed ratification, interpreted the contract clause essentially the same way as Wilson and Madison but saw different implications. It would, Martin declared, prevent the states from stopping "the wealthy creditor and the moneyed man from totally destroying the poor, though industrious debtor." The Virginian Richard Henry Lee made only passing (and approving) reference to the prohibitions of paper money and tender laws in his celebrated anti-Federalist tract *Letters from the Federal Farmer;* he apparently thought the contract clause was insufficiently different from those restrictions to warrant notice.[21]

A considerably different construction was placed on the contract clause by anti-Federalists in the ratifying conventions of Virginia and North Carolina. In Virginia, Patrick Henry and George Mason interpreted the clause as applying to public as well as private obligations, and they objected that the clause thus might require the redemption of old Continental bills of credit, which had depreciated to a thousand for one and had long since ceased circulating. Since $200 million in such bills had been issued, Henry and Mason argued that the ensuing tax burden would bankrupt the country. Madison and others insisted—not to the anti-Federalists' satisfaction—that public obligations were covered by Article V (declaring public debts "as valid" under the Constitution as they had been under the Articles of Confederation) and were unaffected by Article I, Section 10.[22]

North Carolina anti-Federalists made the same argument as those in Virginia, but they added a twist of their own. North Carolina (like Rhode Island, New York, New Jersey, and South Carolina) had issued paper money and made it legal tender, and obligations payable in that paper had been the basis of large numbers of contracts. The paper-money clause would outlaw that currency, and the legal-tender clause would alter those contracts, whereas the contract clause itself prohibited their impairment. North Carolina Federalists could offer no satisfactory rebuttal, for the last-minute insertion of the clause did in fact create a contradiction. Instead, they argued (with unsound legal reasoning, and contrary to both the sense of the Constitutional Convention and the arguments of Virginia Federalists) that the ban on ex post facto laws meant that only future issues of

---

[21] Wilson and Martin quoted in Elliot, *Debates,* vol. 1, p. 376 and vol. 2, p. 492; Madison in *The Federalist,* No. 44 (New York: Modern Library, 1937), p. 291; Lee quoted in Forrest McDonald, ed., *Empire and Nation: Letters from a Farmer in Pennsylvania,* John Dickinson, *Letters from the Federal Farmer, Richard Henry Lee* (Englewood Cliffs, N.J.: Prentice-Hall, 1962), p. 115.

[22] Elliot, *Debates,* vol. 3, pp. 471-481.

paper money and impairment of future contracts were prohibited.[23]

Notwithstanding the confusion in Virginia and North Carolina, and the general agreement on non-Hamiltonian lines elsewhere, the language of the clause could be reasonably interpreted only in the way Hamilton or Wilson had intended it should be interpreted. The future of contract law in America had been writ, and it had been writ large and clear.

Open-Ended Constitutional Provisions: Taxes and the Public Debts

There remains the matter of the Constitution's provisions regarding taxes and the public debts. Despite the avid attention of many delegates to the interests of their states, the provisions concerning taxes evolved in the convention with surprisingly little friction. The delegates agreed to vest Congress with a full range of taxing powers, limited only by the requirements that taxes be levied solely for national purposes, that they be uniform, that direct taxes be allocated among the states in proportion to their population, and that exports be exempt from taxation. The prohibition of state taxes on imports and exports likewise met little resistance. Even more surprisingly, the taxation clauses did not evoke much opposition in the contests over ratification. Some grumbled vaguely that taxes would be oppressively high; occasionally there was an outburst of Bolingbrokean rhetoric about the evils of excises and the infinity of noxious collectors they bred; somewhat more frequently, anti-Federalists argued that the Constitution should have carried over the Confederation's system of imposing requisitions on the states instead of allowing direct taxes as a supplement to imports and excises. It was generally believed that import duties and excise taxes would produce most of the government's needed revenues, and that resorts to direct taxation would be rare.

Agreement on how to provide for the public debts was less easily reached. When the matter was first broached, a number of delegates expressed dissatisfaction with the phrasing and the subject was dropped. It came up again a month later with similar results. Four delegates proposed that Congress be empowered to assume payment of the state debts as well as the Continental debts; another favored assumption but thought specific authorization was unnecessary; another—Elbridge Gerry of Massachusetts, who owned more than

---

[23] Ibid., vol. 4, pp. 156-157, 168-175.

$50,000 in Continental securities—insisted that Continental debts be provided for but not state debts. Gouverneur Morris argued that it was not enough to *empower* Congress to provide for the debts; Congress should be *required* to do so. The convention unanimously adopted his motion that Congress "*shall* discharge the debts and fulfil the engagements of the U States." The next day, however, Pierce Butler of South Carolina delivered a diatribe against "blood-suckers who had speculated on the distresses of others"; Butler insisted that provision be made for discriminating between original creditors and speculators, and he served notice that he would move for a reconsideration. After two days of reconsideration, to cool tempers, Edmund Randolph of Virginia proposed the neutral wording that, with minor modifications, was approved in the finished Constitution: "All Debts contracted and Engagements entered into, before the Adoption of this Constitution, shall be as valid against the United States under this Constitution, as under the Confederation." [24]

That method of dealing with the emotion-laden issue of the public debts—in essence, by passing the buck to the First Congress—accomplished its purpose, for the question was not frequently argued during the contests over ratification. Unfortunately, it also obscured the framers' intentions as to how the public debt should figure in the future course of American economic development. It is possible, however, to reconstruct the attitudes of most of the delegates.

What Alexander Hamilton had in mind is obvious. From his point of view it was an advantage that the Constitution was not specific, for (as I shall make clear in a moment) he saw the public debt as the material from which an institutional system of monetized private credit could be created. Among his fellow delegates at the Constitutional Convention, perhaps five or six shared that vision: Robert and Gouverneur Morris, probably Rufus King and James Wilson, and possibly George Clymer and Thomas Fitzsimons of Pennsylvania. Another ten delegates would give strong support to Hamilton's system when it came before the First Congress. In other words, about seventeen of the fifty-five members of the convention—fewer than a third—viewed, or were persuaded to view, the constitutional provisions regarding public debts as the instrument for the creation of a capitalistic order. On the other hand, thirteen delegates indicated either during the convention, while opposing ratification, or by their later opposition in the First Congress, that they were hostile to that view. The views of the remaining twenty-five delegates

[24] Farrand, *Records*, vol. 2, pp. 46-47, 322, 326ff., 352, 355-356, 368, 377, 382, 392, 400, 408, 412-414.

cannot be ascertained, but from what is known of them it seems probable that all but six or eight would have been part of the opposition.[25]

Other Matters Deferred to Congress

The public debt was not the only potentially divisive issue the convention avoided by passing the buck to the First Congress. The Constitution was left uncompleted in several other crucial areas as well: the Bill of Rights, the appointment and removal powers of the president, the constitution of the judiciary, the makeup and responsibilities of the executive departments. In each of these areas the work of the First Congress amounted to a continuation of the labors of the Constitutional Convention.

The framers' wisdom in deferring these key decisions was, for the most part, promptly confirmed. Unfettered by the need to obtain popular ratification of their measures, the members of the First Congress responded swiftly and decisively to the challenge. Only in regard to money matters—my concern here—did they prove divided and uncertain.

In its first session, Congress enacted two necessary pieces of fiscal legislation, a tariff and the act establishing the Treasury Department. In the debate over the tariff, some representatives sought special protection for the interests of their constituents, some aimed at achieving political goals, and some worked to incorporate mercantilistic principles. As a result, though the act laid the foundations for the revenue system that would be the government's main source of funds for more than a century, it was a veritable textbook example of poorly crafted legislation. As the exasperated collector of

---

[25] The attitude of the Morrises is implicit in Hamilton's consultation of them in preparation for his first "Report on the Public Credit"; see Syrett, *Hamilton Papers*, vol. 6, pp. 54-59, 62-63. Wilson's attitude is inferred from his intimacy with the Morrises, King's from his intimacy with Hamilton, and Clymer's and Fitzsimons's (as well as King's and Robert Morris's) from the strong support they gave Hamilton's system in Congress. The attitude of the second group (which included John Langdon of New Hampshire, Gerry and Caleb Strong of Massachusetts, Johnson, Roger Sherman, and Oliver Ellsworth of Connecticut, William Paterson of New Jersey, George Read of Delaware, George Washington, and Pierce Butler of South Carolina) is also inferred from such support. Of the opponents, John Lansing and Robert Yates of New York, Luther Martin and John Francis Mercer of Maryland, and Mason opposed the Constitution; eight others (Nicholas Gilman of New Hampshire, Richard Bassett of Delaware, Daniel Carroll of Maryland, Madison, Hugh Williamson and Richard Dobbs Spaight of North Carolina, and Abraham Baldwin and William Few of Georgia) fought against Hamilton's system in the First Congress.

the port of Baltimore described it, the law was muddled, impracticable, and contradictory, "the most complicated and embarrassing of anything that has employed my attention." [26]

Debate over the Treasury Department reflected the intense distrust many Americans had of modern fiscal systems. Fearing the establishment of a corrupt, English-style ministerial system, several representatives urged that the Treasury be headed by a three-man board instead of a single secretary. Others, seeking to ensure that the House control the Treasury, insisted that the secretary be required to report directly to the House rather than to the president; but still others thought that would be to unite the power of the purse with the power of the sword by giving the executive branch control over the legislative. By way of compromise, it was finally agreed that the Treasury, like the other executive departments, would be headed by a single secretary, but that he would not be suffered "to touch a farthing of the public money." Instead, the law provided for an auditor to settle and a comptroller to keep track of public accounts, a register to record them, and a treasurer to hold the money. The secretary, made responsible to both the House and the president, was to recommend policy as well as administer the affairs of his department.[27]

Those arrangements were entirely acceptable to the first secretary of the Treasury. Hamilton conceived his role in the new government as that of a prime minister, and despite the intentions of the congressmen, the legislation made it possible for him to play such a role. The subordinate treasury officers freed the secretary from much routine administrative labor; having his responsibility thus divided freed him from the restricting and extremely laborious demands Washington placed upon the secretaries of state and war. Furthermore, the requirement that he report to the House "respecting all matters referred to him or which shall pertain to his office" gave him the opportunity to initiate legislation—a privilege which, as Washington construed the Constitution, even the president did not have.[28]

[26] Otho H. Williams to Hamilton, October 23, 26, 1789, in Syrett, *Hamilton Papers*, vol. 5, pp. 459, 462.

[27] The debates are reported in Thomas Hart Benton, ed., *Abridgment of the Debates in Congress, from 1789 to 1856* (New York, 1857), vol. 1, pp. 90-94 (May 20, 1789), pp. 109-112 (June 25, 1789); they are summarized in McDonald, *Hamilton*, pp. 131-133.

[28] The statute establishing the Treasury Department and specifying the duties of its officers is in *The Laws of the United States of America* (Philadelphia, 1796), vol. 1, pp. 36-40.

The enactment of Hamilton's fiscal program may justly be regarded both as the completion of the Constitution and as the means by which life was breathed into the document. For that reason, and because it is central to the question at hand, a brief review of Hamilton's system is necessary, together with an analysis of what he intended it to accomplish and what it did accomplish.[29]

Hamilton's Fiscal Program

Hamilton viewed the public debt as a means of bringing about a social revolution. He proposed to use it to establish a system in which the value of all things would be set in the marketplace and measured in money—and in so doing, to erect a social order in which success, status, and power would derive from merit and industry rather than, as in the existing scheme of things, from inherited wealth or social position. By institutionalizing the rewarding of industry and the punishment of idleness, he would rouse his countrymen from their "voluptuous indolence" and stimulate them to do the work that would make themselves rich and their nation great.

The first step in Hamilton's grand undertaking was to monetize the public debt. Though a number of congressmen had come to think along those lines by the end of 1789, most had something quite different in view: They simply wanted the debt extinguished in the simplest, easiest, and most expeditious way possible, provided that the means were consistent with national honor and justice to the creditors. Several, indeed, wanted to extinguish it by means that were not consistent with honor and justice, including repudiating all or part of the debt, devaluing it, buying it at deflated prices, and discriminating against present holders of public securities if they were not the original creditors. A goodly number of congressmen were therefore surprised when Hamilton, in his first "Report on the Public Credit," did not suggest ways of paying the debt, at par or otherwise, but instead proposed that it be funded. That is, Congress should provide for regular interest payments by setting up a permanent appropriation of essentially mortgaged revenues, rather than making annual appropriations, and the question of retiring the principal of the debt should be left entirely to the discretion of government. Hamilton made his aims specific: "It is a well known fact," he said, "that in countries in which the national debt is properly funded, and an object of established confidence, it answers most of

---

[29] This interpretation and the account which follows are developed in full in McDonald, *Hamilton*.

the purposes of money." The only options facing the United States, he continued, were "whether the public debt, by a provision for it on true principles, shall be rendered a *substitute* for money; or whether, by being left as it is, or by being provided for in such a manner as will wound those principles, and destroy confidence, it shall be suffered to continue, as it is, a pernicious drain of our cash from the channels of productive industry." [30]

Hamilton's proposal was as follows. The foreign debt (about $11 million, owed to the court of France and to bankers of Holland) would be placed on a regular interest-paying basis and, as principal payments came due, refinanced in the Netherlands. The domestic debt would be refinanced on a different basis. Holders of the outstanding public securities of various sorts (amounting to about $63 million, including $21 million in state debts) would be invited to subscribe to a new loan by exchanging their old paper for new government securities. The new securities, to be assigned to subscribers by a complex formula, would bear different rates of interest: Some paid 6 percent, some paid 3 percent, and some paid no interest for ten years and 6 percent thereafter. The net effective interest rate on the whole debt would be just over 4 percent—which meant that, since the old debt bore 6 percent and since no provision would be made for redeeming the principal, the face value of the old debt was being scaled down by a third. Compensation for the reduced interest was offered in the form of public lands and also increased security. Creditors who chose not to subscribe to the new loan (at first, about a fifth of the total) could retain their old securities and continue to be entitled to their 6 percent interest, but they were not eligible for funds from the permanent appropriation.

All these features, Hamilton believed, would help raise the market value of the new securities. To facilitate the rise, he proposed to establish a "sinking fund," whose purpose was not to retire the debt but to buy and sell public securities on the open market, with the intention of stabilizing the market prices of securities at their par value.

The genius of the system lay in Hamilton's understanding of the nature of money. Money is whatever people believe is money and use as money; as Hamilton put it, "opinion" is the soul of it. If it became fixed in the public mind that government securities were equal in value to and readily interchangeable with gold and silver, people would accept the securities in most transactions as the equivalent of "money," and therefore they would *be* money.

[30] "Report on the Public Credit," in Syrett, ed., *Hamilton Papers*, vol. 6, pp. 70-72.

After a long, acrimonious, and complex debate, Hamilton's proposals were enacted into law on August 4, 1790, with only minor modifications. The result was the almost instantaneous transformation of the public debt from a paralyzing economic liability into highly liquid capital. Moreover, an enormous store of new capital was created in the bargain: the market value of the entire domestic public debt a few months before Hamilton took office had been around $15 million, and by the end of 1790 it was around $45 million. During the next two years, a second transformation took place. Forty new corporations—as many as had been chartered in the colonial and Confederation periods combined—were created; nine for banks, which further multiplied the supply of capital, and the remainder for manufacturing and canal companies. Public securities, sold or pledged abroad, furnished almost all the capital for these ventures.

Meanwhile, Hamilton had proposed and Congress had enacted the next phase of his plan, the establishment of the Bank of the United States.[31] The key feature of the banking system was the way it used the public debt as the basis for the nation's currency. The bank's stock was to be sold to investors, who could pay for up to four-fifths of their subscriptions in government securities at par—which incidentally increased the market value of the securities. Against its total capital of $8 million in 6 percent securities and $2 million in specie, the bank could circulate $10 million in notes which, together with the notes of the state-chartered banks, would serve as the country's principal medium of exchange. Basing the currency on bank notes instead of gold and silver had profound consequences. The crucial characteristic of banking currency is that it is money created in the present, not out of past savings but out of the expectation of future income. Furthermore, because it was inherent in Hamilton's system that money and capital were interchangeable, the government could create capital as well as money by institutionalizing future expectations. This meant that the nation's economic development could be financed on credit without the need for collateral: The collateral was the future itself.

The bill to establish the Bank of the United States met with a celebrated constitutional debate. Madison pointed out that the Constitutional Convention had considered and rejected a proposal to give Congress power to charter corporations, and he argued that failure to grant that power meant the convention had intended for

[31] "Report on a National Bank," ibid., vol. 7, pp. 236-342.

it to remain exclusively with the states. The argument was disingenuous: Madison neglected to mention that it was he who had proposed the motion to grant the power, that the issue had been confused, that some members had thought Congress would have the power without specific authorization, and that (like many another matter) the subject had been left to Congress lest being too specific create unnecessary opposition to ratification. Jefferson's opinion against the constitutionality of the bank, though destined to become the classic statement of the doctrine of strict construction, was mainly just a shorter and less persuasive version of Madison's arguments, spiced by a soupçon of legal mumbo-jumbo.[32]

Hamilton's rebuttal was devastating, profound, and conclusive. To anyone wishing to understand what the Constitutional Convention had wrought—whatever it had intended to do or thought it was doing—his opinion on the constitutionality of the bank is indispensable reading. The convention's crucial action was the very establishment of a government, for from that action a great deal else necessarily flowed. "Every power vested in a Government," Hamilton pointed out, "is in its nature *sovereign*, and includes by *force* of the *term*, a right to employ all the means requisite, and fairly *applicable* to the attainment of the ends of such power; and which are not precluded by restrictions & exceptions specified in the constitution; or not immoral, or not contrary to the essential ends of political power."[33]

Given such extensive powers, and given the Constitution's open-ended language regarding matters of public finance, the First Congress had been vested with the awesome responsibility and opportunity of choosing what kind of political economy the nation would have. Although most Americans probably would have chosen otherwise, Congress chose the Hamiltonian way. The United States would be built under a government-channeled, government-encouraged, and sometimes government-subsidized system of private enterprise for personal profit.

From the Founding to the Present

The choices made between 1787 and 1791 guided the course of American development for more than a century and a half. During

---

[32] For Madison's argument, see Benton, *Abridgment of Debates*, vol. 1, pp. 274-278, 306-308 (February 2, 8, 1791); for Jefferson's, Julian P. Boyd, ed., *The Papers of Thomas Jefferson*, 21 vols. to date (Princeton, N.J.: Princeton University Press, 1950–), vol. 19, pp. 275-280.

[33] "Opinion on the Constitutionality of an Act to Establish a Bank," in Syrett, ed., *Hamilton Papers*, vol. 8, p. 98.

that time the American nation marched to greatness as the richest, freest, and most powerful political society in the history of the world—a beacon light unto mankind. After that began another and sadder story. Both stories are beyond the scope of this essay, but we do have room to suggest their general outlines.

To do so we must start, as people were fond of saying in the eighteenth century, with first principles; with the Founding Fathers' basic assumptions about the nature of humankind and society. In regard to both political and economic life, the Founders' first premise was that man is governed not by virtue or reason but by his passions, meaning his desires for self-gratification, and is happiest when left alone to pursue those desires. The secondary premise of the syllogism, however, was different in politics and economics. In politics, the secondary premise was that none are safe in pursuing their desires for self-gratification unless all are restrained by a government of laws. The conclusion was that government is therefore necessary to provide the maximum of liberty consistent with the safety and well-being of both individuals and society as a whole. In economics, the secondary premise was that men are interdependent and, in pursuit of self-gratification, find it necessary to gratify others. As Adam Smith put it, "It is not from the benevolence of the butcher, the brewer or the baker that we expect our dinner, but from their regard of their own interest."[34] The conclusion was that the material prosperity of a society will therefore be best served if all its members are at liberty, under law, to pursue their personal gain.

The Constitution and the Hamiltonian system of political economy embodied these two principles in America's fundamental law. Now, the idea of fundamental law can be understood most readily if one conceives of political and economic activity as games played in accordance with rules: Fundamental law is the rule book, defining the objects of the game and specifying how it is to be played. The Constitution was the rule book for government, the Hamiltonian system for the economy. The political and economic games as played in America, however, differ from ordinary games in two key respects. One is that they are open-ended rather than zero-sum: There can be many winners, and there need not be any losers. The other is that the games are interrelated: Winners in the money game can influence the course of the political game, and winners in the political game can change the rules of the money game.

---

[34] Adam Smith, *The Wealth of Nations*, condensed and edited by Bruce Mazlish (Indianapolis, Ind.: The Bobbs-Merrill Company, 1961), p. 15.

These arrangements proved to be remarkably stable; they remained essentially intact despite wars, territorial expansion, population growth, and a technological revolution that transformed the world into something the Founding Fathers would not have recognized. There were changes in the system, to be sure. The Supreme Court under Roger Brooke Taney interpreted the Constitution differently from the Marshall Court, and Taney's successors interpreted it differently still. The Jeffersonians and Jacksonians attacked and temporarily destroyed the Hamiltonian fiscal apparatus, and the Hamilton-Jefferson feud was, in different forms, repeatedly refought in the twentieth century. Still, as long as the American story was a success story, the rules of the game changed mainly to expand the base of players who could compete successfully; the object of the game remained the same. This continued to be true even through Franklin Roosevelt's New Deal and Harry Truman's Fair Deal. Despite the stretching of the Constitution during those administrations, the federal government over which Dwight Eisenhower presided in the 1950s was still recognizably the one over which George Washington had presided in the 1790s; and despite Roosevelt's and Truman's rhetorical attacks on big business, both were seeking to make capitalism work more effectively and equitably, not to destroy it.

Then came the sadder story.[35] In the 1960s the federal government, under the presidency of Lyndon Johnson and the chief justiceship of Earl Warren, launched a massive, all-out effort to extend the American system of political economy far beyond the limits of what was possible. The fruits of those efforts, besides a general loss of faith in the system when the efforts failed, were a Supreme Court that legislates rather than adjudicates and a metastasized federal bureaucracy. The Court, driven by a mindless compulsion to legislate equality, has changed not just the rules but the very object of the government game, which was to provide as much individual liberty as is compatible with the public safety. Into the bargain it has all but abolished the idea of a written constitution that means what it says. The bureaucracy, driven by a mindless compulsion to run everything, has changed not just the rules but the very object of the economic

---

[35] The literature on what follows is large. I would recommend, among others, Forrest McDonald, *The Phaeton Ride: The Crisis of American Success* (New York: W. W. Norton & Company, 1974); Raoul Berger, *Government by Judiciary: The Transformation of the Fourteenth Amendment* (Cambridge: Harvard University Press, 1977); William E. Simon, *A Time for Truth* (New York: Reader's Digest Press, 1978); and the files of *National Review*, *Commentary*, and *Harper's* for the relevant years.

game, which was private pursuit of personal gain. Into the bargain it has all but abolished the idea that rewards should be commensurate with effort as measured by values set in the marketplace. Between them, the Court and the bureaucracy have made government as oppressive and arbitrary as under a feudal baron. Nor does the resemblance to feudalism end there. Government regulations are leading inexorably to zero economic growth (a goal that a number of bureaucratic agencies actively espouse); zero economic growth necessarily would make economic activity a zero-sum game; and that in turn would lock people into the relative socioeconomic position into which they were born. Along the way, the "exploitation rate"—the percentage of a producer's output that is taken away from him—reaches more than 40 percent in taxes alone. That is as much as the exploitation rate under serfdom, and twice the rate under antebellum Southern slavery.

To conclude: The Constitution was not originally designed to establish capitalism in America, but constitutional government and capitalism became inextricably intertwined at the outset. They were born together, they lived together, they prospered together, and—unless we return to first principles, and soon—they will die together.

4

The Constitution, Capitalism, and the Need for Rationalized Regulation

Walter Dean Burnham

Every successful system of government can be said, almost axiomatically, to be in the business of promoting the well-being of whatever group or groups hold the most power in the society over which it presides. At the broadest possible level, the state—any state—fulfills three essential functions. First, it defends the basic needs and interests of those who control the means of production within the society in question. Closely associated with this is the second function of the state: achieving legitimacy for itself and ensuring social harmony. This function involves the remarkable fact, brooded on by political theorists since time immemorial, that somehow the state—which is organized force—becomes an engine of moral *authority*, and its rule is accepted in the main by those who are subject to it. Finally, no state can survive if it cannot adequately defend itself, and the dominant powers in the economy and society, from external attack.

To assert all this, and particularly to stress the fit between a given political regime and its constitutional structure on the one hand and the group that controls the means of production on the other, is no simple exercise in vulgar Marxism. The state, after all, is more than (and different from) a mere executive committee of the ruling class. The tradition among political theorists of positing a centrally important link between the nature and requirements of the economic regime and the character of the political states is of long standing, extending from Aristotle through James Harrington and John Adams. What is striking, however, is not its presence among pre-Marxist theorists, but its tendency to disappear from liberal thought from the eighteenth century onward. Nonliberal thought, and especially Marxist thought, has done us the favor of continuing that tradition (to be sure, for its own tendentious purposes). To assert a central link between the structure and functioning of a political regime and the corresponding economic structure, then, is to risk triteness. It is the nature of the link that warrants consideration.

Capitalism and Constitutions

Although there is only one capitalism, clearly distinct from feudal manorialism or socialism as a mode of production, many different constitutions and political regimes have proved to be compatible with it. Capitalism seems to coexist well enough with parliamentary democracy, with the American separation of powers, with substantial economic activity on the part of the public sector (as in continental Europe), and even with Nazism. The reason so many constitutions have arisen—and many more are possible—is that every country has a unique national history. Capitalism has come into dominance as a mode of production in highly diverse political and historical circumstances.

Just as important, however, is the fact that there have been many capitalisms in each country's history, including ours. To be sure, when one thinks of the economic and political systems of the Soviet Union today, or of Rome, Byzantium, or medieval France, the liberal capitalism with which we are familiar is strikingly distinctive. Yet capitalism as a mode of production has passed through a long historical development in every country where it exists today.

Let us briefly examine the American case. In the United States, the mercantilism of 1800 yielded to the laissez-faire of relatively small firms in the ages of Jackson and Lincoln. This in turn was largely replaced by corporate concentration and trusts by the turn of the century, though the political gospel of laissez-faire continued to dominate both the Constitution, particularly as expounded by the Supreme Court, and the political process until the Great Depression and the advent of the New Deal. All of these changes were going on, furthermore, in the context of a fundamental shift from a predominantly agricultural to an urban-industrial political base. Finally, with the arrival of the New Deal, the modern interventionist state gradually came into full being, producing the political capitalism with which we are so familiar today. This really occurred in two stages: the New Deal proper, lasting until the outbreak of World War II, and the deepening and extension of the political-capitalist state after 1960. Meanwhile, the private sector itself has continually undergone change and expansion. In the 1890s, American capitalism was still largely confined within the national boundaries. But, internationally as well as domestically, the turn of the century was also a turning point in our economic and political development. With the proclamation of the open-door policy in China, the annexation of the Philippines, and the emergence of dollar diplomacy in the Caribbean, American capitalism began its epochal movement abroad. Since World War II, the commanding heights of the American corporate economy have become thoroughly multinational, as our external policies have grown more imperial. Today, we live in a world of interdependence, of superorganization, that would have dumbfounded our liberal-capitalist ancestors.

Yet the American Constitution has survived all these overwhelming changes. In fact, it has so far survived them largely intact. This document was drafted as a frame of government for a society more than 90 percent of whose employed adults worked in agriculture, for an economy that had only one bank—the Bank of New York, founded in 1784—and no city with as many as 100,000 inhabitants, and in a physical setting such that many weeks were required for anyone to cross the Atlantic or to travel overland from Maine to Georgia. It endures to this day, a palimpsest on which all these changes have been written for two centuries. The fact that it has so endured is perhaps even more astounding than the changes themselves.

As the relation between capitalism and the American state is examined, then, two aspects of its history take on particular importance. First is the form of the state specified by the Constitution. Of the advanced industrial countries, all except the United States and France have parliamentary regimes, in which a parliament and a prime minister and cabinet lead the dominant party (or coalition) in the legislature. The system of separated powers, with a president and Congress as political branches and a wide policy-making function for the judicial branch as well, is an American creation. Formally copied by many countries in Latin America and by the Philippines—with practical political results more often than not bizarre and repellent to Americans and their liberal tradition—the system of separated powers has not been adopted by another advanced industrial state.[1] This American uniqueness is more than constitutional, as we shall see. Its costs, in terms of coherent channels for the accumulation of power and for sustained public policy in any field, are notoriously high. It can work as a system of govern-

---

[1] The partial exception is France, of course, with an independently elected powerful president on one hand, and a parliament, cabinet, and prime minister on the other. Space precludes any extended discussion of this anomaly.

ment only in certain contexts; in particular, it requires a high degree of consensus in public opinion.

The notion of the Constitution as a palimpsest is the second point that needs further exploration. This is particularly necessary if we are to follow Aristotle and insist that *the constitution* includes not only the Constitution as a document but the entire network of attitudes, norms, behaviors, and expectations among elites and publics that surround and support the written instrument. For in this larger sense, it is obvious that the constitution has evolved repeatedly and significantly in the course of American history in response to significant changes in context. Reading the written document alone would give little inkling of the extent of these transformations, to which presidents, legislators, judges, political parties, economic interests, and the American people have all vitally contributed.

Yet throughout their mutations, the American Constitution and the broader constitution have never ceased to be linked in an essential—and historically positive—way with capitalism. The changes have been adaptive, not revolutionary. If there have been many capitalisms in the history of the United States, however, an important question immediately presents itself. Could the constitution and the fundamental requirements of the dominant mode of production reach a historical context in which they would come into acute conflict? If so, this would mean that the constitution's capacity to adapt to a new context had innate limits, and that these limits had been reached or passed.

Any constitution may be understood as an organized distribution of political powers, rights and obligations, broadly reflecting the dominant interests and values of the society for which it is designed. The longer it lasts, the better the fit between the structure of political power and these dominant interests and values is likely to be. Throughout most of our history, the American Constitution has appeared to fit well the needs of capitalism and of a society whose system of values is dominated by Lockean, proprietarian liberalism. If the fit between Constitution and capitalism can now seriously be called into question, we might well suspect that some significant change in the political needs of capitalism and its elites is responsible.

A regime based upon the competition of ambition against ambition, and upon a culture deeply suspicious of concentrated power in any form, is a regime that can be expected to have problems with its steering mechanism. These problems, serious enough on occasion in the simpler past, could well take on an altogether greater importance in the superorganized and vulnerable environment that now surrounds capitalism. The possibility thus arises that the traditional American Constitution and the requirements of capitalism in its multinational-imperial phase may have come to a parting of the ways. In this essay I shall attempt to address this possibility and some of its implications. Before doing so, however, I must first draw attention to the nature of the Constitution—"the spirit of the laws," in Montesquieu's phrase—and that document's relationship with capitalism in earlier periods of the country's history.

Special Qualities of the United States

What are the most striking peculiarities of the United States as a political, economic, and social system? The sense that the United States is somehow fundamentally different from the Western European matrix from which its white population came is as old as the republic itself. What is the essence of this difference? Many clues to it have been advanced. This is a country that was "born equal" (Hartz); in its formative years it was dominated by the experiences associated with "the Great Frontier" (Webb). Its people, compared with even the most advanced European populations, have been a "people of plenty" (Potter); or, as Werner Sombart said in explaining the failure of socialism to take root in the United States, "All socialist utopias have come to grief on roast beef and apple pie." In sum, the United States was founded at a specific *time*, by specific *populations* derived from a much wider potential range of European peoples, in a specific *context* of physical geography and potential resources *isolated* from other advanced societies (notably from the European-British mother-matrix). It therefore was and is, in Louis Hartz's terms, a "fragment culture" and a "fragment society"; and these probably are the two most important terms that can be used to describe it in comparison with any part of Europe.[2]

The first of these points worth considering is the time factor. The white populations that settled the American Atlantic seaboard came overwhelmingly from Great Britain in the seventeenth and early eighteenth centuries. That is, they arrived long after the end of the

[2] Louis Hartz, *The Liberal Tradition in America* (New York: Harcourt, Brace & World, 1955), p. 309; Walter Prescott Webb, *The Great Frontier* (Austin: University of Texas Press, 1962); David Potter, *People of Plenty* (Chicago: University of Chicago Press, 1954); Werner Sombart, *Warum gibt es in den Vereinigten Staaten keinen Sozialismus?* (Tübingen, 1906), trans. and excerpted in John H. M. Laslett and Seymour M. Lipset, *Failure of a Dream?* (New York: Doubleday, 1974), p. 599; Louis Hartz, ed., *The Founding of New Societies* (New York: Harcourt, Brace & World, 1964), pp. 1-122.

Middle Ages and of medieval social relationships in England, but long before the onset of industrialization, and from a country that was economically, politically, and socially the most modern in Europe.

Second, the founding *populations* were virtually entirely white, Protestant, and—with the exception of the Pennsylvania Germans—English speaking. There is of course a vast literature on the relationship between "the Protestant ethic" or Protestantism as a whole and the cultural values supportive of capitalism.[3] Without reviewing this line of argument in detail, it is possible to see how a sociologically modern population—for the most part literate and already inclined by religion, culture, and social class toward an ethics of individual responsibility and self-reliance—would be a fertile seedbed for the liberal capitalist republic that grew up here.

The North American *context* of geography and resources also was virtually ideal for the development of an acquisitive, profit-oriented society based on individual initiative. The environment was there to be mastered and exploited by those with the skills and cultural attributes to do so. Of vital importance as a contextual determinant was the new nation's geographic *isolation*, which influenced its history until 1941 or so. The United States was separated by thousands of miles from any rival powers of serious importance, protected for a century after the Treaty of Ghent (1814) by the British fleet and the balance of power in Europe. In the Western Hemisphere, the United States was incomparably more powerful than any other nation. This point was rudely, but not inaccurately, made by Secretary of State Olney during the Anglo-Venezuelan crisis of 1895: "The United States is practically sovereign on this continent, and its fiat is as law to those subjects to which it confides its interposition." [4]

The characteristic pattern of political development in post-medieval Europe was the creation, over centuries, of the "hard state"—that is, of governments, internally sovereign and relatively autonomous. In most cases, though not in Great Britain, this entailed the destruction of medieval representative institutions and the emergence of dynasties headed by absolute rulers, the last of which

---

[3] The classic theses were presented by Max Weber, *The Protestant Ethic and the Spirit of Capitalism* (New York: Scribners, 1958), and Richard H. Tawney, *Religion and the Rise of Capitalism* (New York: Harcourt, Brace, 1926). For a variety of more contemporary views, see S. N. Eisenstadt, ed., *The Protestant Ethic and Modernization: A Comparative View* (New York: Basic Books, 1968).

[4] Quoted in Samuel Flagg Bemis, *A Diplomatic History of the United States* (New York, Holt, 1936), p. 418.

(Russia, Austria-Hungary, and Prussia-Germany) persisted until as late as 1917 or 1918. The emergence of the hard state, with its elaborate, rational public bureaucracy and—later still—its grounding in universal suffrage and parliamentary government, was largely attributable to two factors. The first was the struggle within the state among classes and other large-scale social formations, each attempting to capture control of the state's power resources to smash its opponents. Capitalism in such states was contested more or less bitterly as it came into being by the Church, the aristocracy, and their counterparts, the peasantry. Later it was contested no less bitterly by an alienated proletariat and the revolutionary socialist intellectuals who espoused the proletariat's cause, giving organized form to its social demands.

The second and equally indispensable incentive to the creation of the hard state was the struggle between states. The American social critic Randolph Bourne put it succinctly: "War is the health of the state." The European matrix was not one in which any nation could ever claim to be "practically soverign on this continent." [5] It was, rather, populated with many rival sovereignties of more or less equal power—and more or less equal, and constant, anxiety about defense. Bismarck, seeing that Germany could not be unified without violence, first overthrew the liberal parliamentary opposition to absolutism within Prussia, then overthrew Prussia's external enemies. The matter, he pointed out, would "not be resolved by speeches and majority decisions . . . but by iron and blood." [6]

The contrast with the United States throughout most of its history could hardly be greater. As late as the mid-1930s, the U.S. Army contained scarcely more men under arms than the hundred thousand to which the Treaty of Versailles limited Germany. Isolation made any larger standing army unnecessary, apart from the temporary exigencies of the Civil War and World War I, until the old-world balance of power finally came to an end in 1940.

The effect of America's unique historical position on its domestic development can be put into four words: no feudalism, no socialism. With the partial (and only partial) exception of the sectional crisis that grew into the Civil War, European-style struggles within the state or over control of the state never happened in this country. As Louis Hartz has correctly pointed out, the theory of social conflict

[5] Randolph S. Bourne, *War and the Intellectuals: Collected Essays, 1915-1919*, ed. Carl Resek (New York: Harper & Row, 1964), p. 71.
[6] Otto von Bismarck, *Die Gesammelten Werke* [Collected Works], 19 vols. (Friedrichsruh, 1924-1932), vol. 10, p. 140.

out of which the Founders constructed the Constitution of 1787 did not apply to American conditions. If it had, the Constitution would have been overthrown within a generation after 1787.[7] It is easy to make too much of the American consensus, and not a few analysts have overstated its extent and power. Nevertheless, the country's relative freedom from internal strife has been an important factor in its history. The First Amendment ratified a social condition which precluded internal religious struggles from ever becoming the axis around which national politics revolved, as they are in, say, Northern Ireland. In economics, the absence of any social structures or interests inimical to capitalism, coupled with a uniquely favorable history, location, and resource base, ensured that the question whether capitalism ought to be the nation's economic system was never debated as such, however bitter the struggles between the winners and the losers created by that system might become on occasion. In politics, the absence of struggles within the state of the European sort, plus a Lockean-individualistic political culture and a unique physical and social context, critically limited the consolidation of the American state from the outset. Instead, voluntary cooperation and self-regulation were continually stressed as the basic principles of sociopolitical action. Our historic isolation from credible external threats likewise removed this primordial incentive to state building along European lines.[8]

Taken all in all, the relation between capitalism and the Constitution in America has been defined chiefly by the fact that capitalism as a dominant mode of production has lacked any sustained challenge from any serious organized social force to its right to exist. Every economic system without exception is associated with a characteristic hegemony in the political culture and consciousness of the society that it dominates. Karl Marx understood this point in his own way when he observed that the ruling ideas of every age are the ideas of its ruling class. Ideas that bolster the existing order of things are what sociologists call "pattern-maintenance" arising from "political socialization," which Marxist thinkers describe as "repro-

---

[7] This is, throughout, the argument advanced by Louis Hartz in *The Liberal Tradition in America*. He observes, "The solution the constitutionalists offered to the frightful conflicts they imagined was a complicated scheme of checks and balances which it is reasonable to argue only a highly united nation could make work at all. Delay and deliberate confusion in government become intolerable in communities where men have decisive social programs that they want to execute" (p. 85).

[8] Samuel P. Huntington, *Political Order in Changing Societies* (New Haven: Yale University Press, 1968), pp. 93-139.

duction" of social relations. They are propagated by social institutions—the school, the press, the pulpit, the patriotic ceremony (the presidential inaugural address, for example), and above all the family—whose chief task it is. Taken together, these are the means by which hegemony is diffused. The ideas themselves form the substantive content of hegemony, a content that is specific to each country and each historical era.

In Europe, since at least the end of the Middle Ages and the beginning of the Protestant Reformation in the sixteenth century, all hegemonies have been problematic, since all have been bitterly contested. Capitalist-bourgeois ideology, and the dominant class whose interests it most perfectly reflects, has been involved in a continuous two-front war against important Old Conservative remnants on the right and socialism on the left. This war, as usual, reflects another war: the struggle of bourgeois elitist groups to capture the state, in order to smash the hold of nobility and church on society and economy, and their subsequent struggle to preserve themselves against attacks from the lower orders of the industrial society which they had created. In America, on the other hand, hegemony has been uncontested. It has rested squarely upon four cardinal values: property, liberty, democracy, and religion. The pervasive hold of this liberal tradition on the American public mind, more than any other single factor, explains the most extraordinary fact of American political history: the most dynamic society and economy on earth have coexisted with the most antique and undeveloped constitutional structure to be found in any Western country. It follows that, when we look at the Constitution in either the narrower documentary sense or in the broader Aristotelian sense, we may well be looking—at least historically—at the ideal capitalist state.

The Ideal Capitalist State

However much capitalism may have changed in the course of its existence, it has always stressed that the chief energizing principle of human action is the individual's pursuit of rational self-interest, with the least possible interference from others. In its early, revolutionary stage, capitalism and its protagonists sought an end to feudal privilege and to all artificial and collectivist barriers to the liberation of the individual. The individual's pursuit of rational self-interest, it was argued, would release unimagined productive energies, benefiting society as a whole. The political system, accordingly, should not be grounded in organic collective relationships among classes, estates, and castes. It must be grounded, according to eighteenth-century bourgeois liberal thought, in a social contract made among autonomous individuals according to the basic capitalistic organizational principle of limited liability.

What then, would be the ideal form for a liberal capitalist state to adopt? In the first place, it should be a republic rather than a monarchy (a revolutionary enough idea in the world of 1787). The republic should be grounded in "the people" as a whole for its legitimacy. Even if not explicitly, the basic rationale of the republic as a system of government should be the theory of the social compact. The individual, with his rights to life, liberty, and property, is at the center. Protecting these is what the system is all about. To provide protection, governmental powers should be separated both vertically and horizontally—vertically by being divided between a central and many local governments, horizontally by being divided among branches of the central government—in order to prevent the kind of consolidation that could lead to tyranny. If "the people" as a whole is to be sovereign, and the individual's indefeasible rights are to be proctected, then *internal sovereignty*—the power of any one organ of government to decide conclusively any issue of importance—must be prevented. *External* sovereignty—the central government's power to organize effective foreign policy and armed forces to deal with other states—is of course quite a different matter.

This kind of rhetoric discloses one of the most important characteristics of the ideal system: It is strongly *isolative.* It builds walls between one center of power and another. Even more important, it builds walls between the state as a presumably neutral legatee and civil society. The reality of domination is masked in countless ways from plain view, either as it is reflected in state power or as it exists in the prevailing mode of production.

To summarize, then, the ideal state supporting and supported by liberal capitalism would be one strikingly similar to that with which we are so familiar. The people rule, guided by a higher law and its interpreters. Internal sovereignty is denied. The state is isolated—not only practically but in the citizens' consciousness—from the economy and civil society, existing solely to facilitate the free play of forces in both. The Constitution also, of course, sets up multiple institutional barriers within government itself, with the consequence that a huge amount of energy is expended in dealing first with boundary or jurisdictional problems before anything else can be decided, and the additional consequence that courts play a more extensive political role in the United States than in any other country.

The tendency toward isolating and boundary setting is strongly marked in the culture—in the mystique that surrounds the "rule of law," for example, often making it into a brooding omnipresence in the skies, and in the tendency to insist upon a clear-cut distinction between "public" and "private." But it is reflected peculiarly in the Constitution itself. If scholars such as Charles H. McIlwain and Samuel P. Huntington are to be believed, the result is an organization of political power which has marked late-medieval characteristics. Huntington, in fact, calls the American regime a "Tudor polity." [9] "In seventeenth-century Europe," Huntington observes in contrast, "the state replaced fundamental law as the source of political authority, and within each state a single authority replaced the many which had previously existed." [10] As a result of the protracted struggles over social, economic, and political fundamentals already alluded to, these states became internally soverign to a degree that was—and is—wholly alien to the American constitutional tradition. In England and elsewhere, the command of the sovereign is the fount of law and political obligation, though the identity of that sovereign has undergone crucial changes in the past several centuries.

The reason a late-medieval political structure could coexist with one of the world's most dynamically evolving economic and social systems is that, in the most fundamental sense, the state did not matter. Struggles to control the state for the purpose of using its organized force to determine fundamental economic, social, and religious arrangements were (save for the Civil War) nonexistent in American political history. Most of the more spectacular political conflicts—say, between conservatism and the New Deal in the 1936 presidential election, or between silver and gold advocates in 1896—were, in this broader sense, sham battles: Armageddon was thought to be at hand, but mistakenly. Afterwards, as before, the primary business of America was business, to a degree inconceivable even in Britain, not to mention continental Europe. Lacking the tremendous European dialectic of conflict extending from the end of the Middle Ages to the Russian Revolution and World Wars I and II, the American political system *did not develop at all.* Even in 1980, with all the many significant (but, I would argue, nondevelopmental) changes in the role and functions of the national government that

[9] Huntington, *Political Order;* cf. Charles H. McIlwain, *The High Court of Parliament and Its Supremacy* (New Haven: Yale University Press, 1910; reprint ed., New York, Arno Press, 1979); Samuel P. Huntington, *Political Order in Changing Societies.*

[10] Huntington, *Political Order,* p. 98.

have occurred over the past half-century, the American Constitution remains a Tudor polity. Political structure remains unconsolidated; individual and corporate liberty are still defended by a dense network of institutional walls; the state still lacks any determinate internal sovereignty.

As Edmund Burke pointed out two centuries ago, however, a polity without the means of change is without the means of its own conservation. If we have not had *developmental* change toward differentiation of functions, consolidation of final decision-making authority, and the rest, surely the American Constitution (and constitution) have undergone *some* form of change. What kinds of changes have brought the political structure up to date? What new stages of capitalist development have appeared in the political economy, and what new forms of social organization? What have been the chief adaptive mechanisms?

The Emergence of Parties

Political parties have been an absolutely essential ingredient of the American constitution. Deplored by the framers of the Constitution, and nowhere mentioned in that document, parties have been a vital counterweight to the dispersion of power caused by what James Madison at one point called "our feudal Constitution." [11] It seems historically clear that even then, political parties channeled power, created bonds, accumulated power, and in general linked the public with the activities of the national government. Before their full institutionalization in the Jackson period, the national government was, in James Sterling Young's words, "at a distance and out of sight." [12] This changed radically in the 1830s. Parties mobilized the potential electorate, entertained it when other entertainments were hard to come by, and concentrated its attention on issues and personalities far removed from the day-to-day life of urban neighborhood, county seat, or farm. In addition, parties bridged the institutional chasms created by the Constitution's vertical and horizontal fragmentation of political power. In the golden age of the traditional American party system—roughly 1830 to 1900—politicians had to work together as teams if any of their major purposes were to be realized. The bonds of striving together against determined opposi-

[11] Quoted in William A. Williams, *The Contours of American History* (Cleveland and New York: World, 1961), p. 149.
[12] *The Washington Community, 1800-1828* (New York: Columbia University Press, 1966), pp. 13-37.

tion were never closer than in the relationships between Abraham Lincoln on one hand and the congressional leadership and the wartime governors of the Northern states on the other, to cite just one example.

To the extent that these bondings worked, and party became, in V. O. Key's expression, "the solvent of federalism," [13] the channels of support and demand that parties created made it possible for leaders to accumulate power. This was true even though this accumulation of power required rather special contextual circumstances—and even though, at that, the constitutional framework always placed major limits on it. In fact, a dispassionate reading of American political history reveals that the Madisonian Constitution *by itself* was a radically defective instrument of government right from the beginning. It could not function to protect the most primordial aspects of the national interest without the counterweight of parties; and the national government that grew out of it could not retain the required popular support or respect without that counterweight. Pure Madisonian constitutional arrangements were never adequate to provide the national government with the power resources it needed to function as a national government. Something else was always required, and political parties provided it. Without them, hyperpluralism runs rampant, the fragmentation of political power has no counterbalance, and political paralysis is the inevitable consequence. In our own time, political parties have undergone radical decay. This is a genuinely ominous development for the future of the American constitution.

Political Realignments

The history of parties as a constituent part of the American polity cannot, of course, be understood apart from the limits on parties' potential that are imposed by the Constitution's (and constitution's) constraints. The comparative archaism of our institutional arrangements, their lack of development, coexists with the enormously dynamic course of capitalism's development in the American economy and society—a coexistence made possible by the uncontested hegemony capitalism has historically enjoyed in the United States. Still, conflict between winners and losers under capitalism continually goes on, and with time, the losers inevitably gravitate toward politics and the state in their search to redress the balance. New demands corre-

[13] *American State Politics* (New York: Alfred A. Knopf, 1956), pp. 34-40.

spondingly arise. They, and those who raise them, collide head-on with a political structure that is already fairly completely organized, and whose politicians have no particular incentive to respond to new demands. A perennial gap exists between static politics and the social and political effects of rapid, autonomously generated change in economy and society. Eventually the gap becomes so wide—so many new interests and needs remain unrepresented by the old politics, from sectors of the capitalist elite to major sectors of the American electorate—that some triggering event produces a political explosion and a dramatic and rapid reorganization of American politics as a whole.

These *critical realignments* have been described in many ways. I have called them elsewhere the American "surrogate for revolution." [14] Their explosive, dramatic character arises from the underlying characteristics of the constitutional system as a whole: the constant intrinsic tendency for the dynamic socioeconomic base to slide out from under the static political superstructure until the growing maladaptation between the two causes a major crisis. In the transformations that follow, not only do voting patterns change drastically, but new elites emerge into political dominance, new policy agendas take over, and a new variant of Lockean liberalism evolves in the broader culture, bringing it up to date and shaping public norms and expectations accordingly.

Emergency Measures

Occasionally a crisis is—or appears to be—so extreme that the state resorts to a more drastic way of adapting to it. This is the "constitutional dictatorship," to use Clinton Rossiter's phrase. [15] Very simply, whatever parts of the Constitution seem to stand in the way of national survival are practically declared out of operation for the duration of the emergency. It is the chief executive who becomes the "constitutional dictator," and he establishes precedents based on the old truth that necessity knows no law. Nor, as a rule, does the Supreme Court attempt to challenge him until the crisis has clearly passed. The list of Lincoln's violations of the letter of the Constitution in the 1861 crisis is very long: Among many other things, he increased the number of officers and men in the regular Army and

[14] Walter Dean Burnham, *Critical Elections and the Mainsprings of American Politics* (New York: W. W. Norton & Co., 1970).

[15] Clinton Rossiter, *Constitutional Dictatorship* (New York: Harcourt, Brace, & World, 1963).

Navy, suspended the writ of habeas corpus from Washington to New York, and used military power to disperse the Maryland legislature and arrest some of its members. The confinement of West Coast American citizens of Japanese ancestry in relocation camps from 1942 to 1945 is a conspicuous example of deprivation of liberty and property without due process of law under emergency conditions.

These delegations of power to the executive in a crisis are bound to continue, for in the existing constitutional order there is no practical alternative. One of the most telling cases in point was Congress's delegation to President Nixon of sweeping powers to cope with the oil-embargo emergency in late 1973, precisely when the congressional machinery was being geared up to impeach him in the wake of the Watergate revelations. It goes without saying that if there is ever a major military crisis involving the United States and the Soviet Union, or a serious disruption in the flow of Middle Eastern oil to the advanced industrial countries, constitutional dictatorship will again be the order of the day.

The Metamorphosis of the Mid-1900s

What does all this tell us about the problematic relationship between capitalism and the Constitution at present?

As long ago as 1941, the eminent constitutional scholar Edward S. Corwin observed that a fundamental change was occurring in American political and constitutional history. The traditional American Constitution, he argued, depended for its survival on two conditions which had disappeared or were disappearing in his day, and have entirely vanished forty years later. The first condition was that the national government have no permanent role in managing or attempting to control the economy. In other words, for things to work as they traditionally had, the isolative barriers between the state and laissez-faire autonomy would have to remain high and largely impenetrable. The second condition was that the United States as a whole have no permanent military or imperial involvement in world affairs—that it remain isolated and thus out of any serious danger of a fatal external attack. With the disappearance of these negative conditions, a whole new chapter in American history was opening. In Corwin's view, it was questionable whether the Constitution could survive long in their absence.[16]

[16] "The Aggrandizement of Presidential Power," in Robert S. Hirschfield, ed., *The Power of the Presidency* (Chicago: Aldine, 1973), pp. 245-258. Orig. title "Some Aspects of the Presidency," in *The Annals*, Nov. 1941, pp. 122-131.

The underlying issues that Corwin identified were obvious enough to conservatives such as Herbert Hoover in the 1930s, but few others were aware of them till the 1960s. The Constitution appeared to be continuing its protections well enough; and even if civil liberties were under serious pressure from time to time (for example, during the McCarthy era at the onset of the cold war), the problems involved did not jeopardize capitalist interests in any visible way—quite the contrary, in fact. The conservatives had essentially denied that the Constitution could be stretched far enough to accommodate the interventionist political capitalism that emerged on the ruins of laissez-faire and still preserve liberty. Events from 1941 until far into the 1960s appeared to have proven them as wrong as Democratic doomsayers had been a century earlier.

Unquestionably, the conservatives of the 1930s, like their predecessors in earlier moments of transition, radically underestimated the Constitution's capacity to adapt to new capitalist circumstances. It was, after all, possible to rewrite the symbolic and operational code of government so that the Lockean individual could become the Lockean group. An entire postwar generation of American political scientists discovered the beauties of pluralism, and the maintenance of a Madisonian balance through the free interplay of organized interests with the political process. But what permitted Corwin's warning of 1941 to go so largely unheeded was the United States' embarkation on yet another frontier experience following World War II. The fear, widespread in business circles and the public around 1945, that the end of the war meant a return to the acute economic stagnation and social stress of the 1930s, proved wholly unfounded. As long ago as the turn of the century, John Hay and other spokesmen of the open-door policy in China and elsewhere had seen overseas economic expansion as the key end-run strategy for bypassing the problem of underconsumption, which already had assumed critical proportions during the slump of the 1890s. World War II temporarily destroyed the competitive position of all other rival capitalisms, European as well as Japanese. American policy, enforced by its immense leverage from 1943 on, opened up formerly closed colonial empires—notably the British—to American economic penetration. The American economy acquired an overwhelming international hegemony. The ascendancy of the dollar as the key medium of international economic exchange was ratified by the Bretton Woods agreement in 1944 and remained the centerpiece of the world economy until President Nixon was forced to abrogate it in 1971.

With American capitalism in a more favorable position in the world than ever before in its history, the domestic economy underwent a boom of unprecedented scope and length. Yet remarkably, and contrary to all pre-Keynesian capitalist economic theory, this major and sustained growth in disposable (after-tax) income was accomplished in the teeth of unprecedented growth in the public sector's taxation of that income and in its share of the total gross national product. This new obtrusiveness on the part of the public sector was partly a consequence of programs designed to smooth out the business cycle and to provide some minimum welfare floor for the poor. From the late 1940s through the mid-1960s, however, the lion's share of the public sector's new income went to traditional expenditures: military spending, the space program, foreign aid and international relations, veterans' benefits. For if World War II had destroyed for the time being the competitive position of rival capitalist systems, it also had brought the United States and "world Communism" (later more narrowly defined as the Soviet Union, as we became friendly with the People's Republic of China) face to face. The United States became the pole of an empire in opposition to the Soviet empire. In response to this situation, particularly after the beginning of the Korean War, a huge and permanent "military Keynesian" component was added to the American economy.

The rising affluence of Americans, the traditional character of most of the growth in the public sector, and the solidification into a cold-war consensus of both public and elite attitudes about the proper role of the United States in world affairs all served to sustain the post–New Deal conversion of the American constitutional system into a "political-capitalist" stance. By the late 1960s, indeed, Richard Nixon was proclaiming that he too was a Keynesian. "The system" seemed to be working splendidly. In international affairs particularly, the cold war gave American foreign and military policy makers a wide latitude to act in "the national interest" as they defined it, and—as we have seen—the Constitution provided no serious obstacles.

Of course, creating and maintaining an empire (even a liberal empire such as the American one) involved continuous and chronic, though not usually acute, crisis. Even before the decay of this empire and of the American political economy became manifest in the 1970s, more than a few critics were expressing alarm about the extent to which the changed context of military and imperial affairs was producing an imperial presidency. This development was no more than Corwin had predicted decades earlier. The presidency feeds on crisis, and when crisis becomes chronic, a permanent change of power relationships within the constitutional structure is almost inevitable.

The End of the Golden Era

What happened in the 1960s and 1970s, then, was perhaps not surprising. The cold war consensus was shattered by the decision of American political elites to intervene directly in the Vietnamese conflict, and by the eruption of widespread dissent against that decision and its consequences. From a historical perspective, the Vietnamese war was a variant of the classic imperial frontier war, analogous to the frequent Roman wars against the Persians in Armenia or the British-Afghan war of 1878–1879. Its failure contributed to a derailment of the "imperial presidency" and a shift to weak successors, as did Richard Nixon's fall from power.

The late 1960s were years of enormous internal ferment, galvanized by racial protests, the women's movement, and other demonstrations of disaffection. Extraordinary declines in popular support for and trust of political leaders dominated public-opinion polls taken between 1966 and 1974, and no serious increase has occurred since.[17] Rancorous hyperpluralism has come to the fore, prompting quite a few scholars who once celebrated pluralism and the Lockean group to proclaim the rise of a "governability crisis" or even "the crisis of democracy."[18] In particular, political parties have taken a terrible beating, to the extent that David S. Broder could argue, with only limited exaggeration, that *The Party's Over*.[19] Popular participation in elections has declined along with popular support for officials, with the decline concentrated especially heavily in the distressed, aging industrial-urban belt of the Northeast, and among those working-class adults who had already participated least to begin with.[20]

---

[17] Though interpretations of course vary, the underlying survey data on this point are overwhelming. See Warren E. Miller, Arthur H. Miller, and Edward J. Schneider, *American National Election Studies Data Sourcebook, 1952-1978* (Cambridge: Harvard University Press, 1980), p. 257.

[18] See Nathan Glazer and Irving Kristol, eds., *The American Commonwealth, 1976* (New York: Basic Books, 1976).

[19] *The Party's Over* (New York: Harper & Row, 1972).

[20] See Walter Dean Burnham, "The Appearance and Disappearance of the American Voter," in American Bar Association, *The Disappearance of the American Voter* (Washington, D.C., 1978), pp. 125-167; Arthur T. Hadley, *The Empty Polling Booth* (Englewood Cliffs, N.J.: Prentice-Hall, 1978), and Everett C. Ladd, Jr., *Where Have All the Voters Gone?* (New York: W. W. Norton & Co., 1978).

There is much truth to the saying that when things are going well, any system will appear to be working, and that when they go ill, any system will seem to be on the verge of bankruptcy. This may be no more than to reiterate, with President Kennedy, that victory has a hundred fathers while defeat is an orphan. Nor is America alone in its present troubles; the political systems of a number of European parliamentary democracies have also run into serious problems, as the economic surplus required to support the postwar welfare state has begun to disappear while its burdens seem increasingly to outweigh its benefits.[21] On the other hand, a shift from a favorable to an unfavorable context is bound to expose the previously hidden weaknesses of any regime. The task, then, is to explain how and why these weaknesses have become manifest.

Complexity and the Need for a Steering Mechanism

The end of the frontier has long been proclaimed and at least as long refuted by unexpected events. In a bygone age whose apparent simplicity prompts acute spasms of nostalgia among Americans today, the autonomous self-regulation on which our political culture and institutional structure are predicated appeared to work with mechanical perfection. Yet big organization of any kind necessarily destroys autonomy over time. As far back as the Progressive era, if not earlier, prescient observers of the American political scene perceived a serious dilemma. Although the growing complexity of corporate capitalism and industrial urbanism necessitated a state with the capacity to steer and manage this complexity, the Madisonian Constitution, even as amended by mass participation and a party system, prevented the state from realizing such a capacity. Planning and coordination had become necessities; the question was not whether but by whom and in whose interests they were to be carried out. At first, it seemed that the largest business corporations could perform this task with only occasional and peripheral assistance from government. The ideal of corporate self-regulation failed, however, in the utter bankruptcy that followed the great crash of 1929. As bitterly as many capitalist elites opposed the New Deal, the state intervened as a permanently involved "senior partner" nevertheless

[21] See Michel Crozier et al., *The Crisis of Democracy: Report on the Governability of Democracies to the Trilateral Commission* (New York: New York University Press, 1975); Walter Dean Burnham, "Great Britain: Death of the Collectivist Consensus?" in Louis Maisel and Joseph Cooper, eds., *Political Parties: Development and Decay* (Beverly Hills, Calif.: Sage Publications, 1978).

because conditions left it (and the Roosevelt elite) no choice. Social stability required intervention, no less than the collective interests of those who owned and managed the means of production.

Yet planning and control require a hard state, one in which power to make decisions and accountability or responsibility for what happens are consolidated insofar as conditions require. It goes without saying that military and imperial pressures point in exactly the same direction, the more urgently so as the initial hegemonic position of the United States in world affairs decays. The need for a hard state can be bypassed so long as international ascendancy continues, and so long as rapidly increasing affluence produces an expanding pie which we can afford to cut in a sloppy manner. It cannot be bypassed for long when the core sectors of the industrial economy at home move into a condition of acute distress, when disposable income declines among wide sectors of the working population, when the empire loses control over access to and supplies and prices of critical raw materials from the third world, and when the geopolitical and directly military threat from the Soviet Union mounts while American superiority disappears. In what Lester Thurow has correctly called the *zero-sum society*, comprehensive public policy is required in some of the most basic areas of our collective lives.[22] We need it in energy, in the so-called reindustrialization of America, in our attempts to balance what we can afford with what is most desirable for national defense, and in countless other areas.

It is axiomatic in a zero-sum situation that the gains of one player in the game match the losses of another player. We cannot evade this stark reality by retreating to the positive-sum assumptions of our historical frontier past, where all players gained, some more rapidly than others. This leaves the state in a dilemma. One of the major tasks of any capitalist state is attempting to achieve social harmony while pursuing and encouraging the accumulation of capital.[23] The policy of growth followed after 1945 by the elites of all the advanced industrial countries, including the United States, presumed that the game would remain positive-sum: that they could use the surplus they gleaned from effectively developing capitalist enterprises to promote legitimacy (and thus harmony) by supporting domestic welfare with large-scale public spending. With the dis-

[22] Lester C. Thurow, *The Zero-Sum Society: Distribution and the Possibilities for Economic Change* (New York: Basic Books, 1980).

[23] For one of the most useful analytic discussions of these two primordial functions of the so-called capitalist state, see James O'Connor, *The Fiscal Crisis of the State* (New York: St. Martin's Press, 1973).

appearance of that surplus and the increasing sickness of industry, however, the game became zero-sum, making it increasingly difficult for the state to work toward accumulating capital and ensuring social harmony at the same time. This situation favors choices on the side of capital accumulation, which means depressing the level of both social and private consumption. Who is going to suffer the losses? By what right should others escape the costs? To what extent, if at all, should public policy be employed—as it often is in wartime—to try to equalize the sacrifice?

As yet, debate over such questions has hardly begun. To the extent that our political economy returns to the stagnant, closed-frontier, zero-sum conditions prevalent in the 1930s, however, it will come. The debate almost certainly also will include an open discussion at some stage of the radical defectiveness of the existing constitution as a framework for creating and sustaining comprehensive social and economic policy. The problems of the Madisonian state are bound to be at the center of any serious effort to reconstruct the well-being of the American capitalist political economy. They could be even more so if and when serious attempts ever were made to replace capitalism with what some would view as a more rational, humane, and effective form of economic and social organization. Whether to restore capitalism or replace it is not so much the issue at present, however, as that we must either decide or decay yet further.

The power to decide, to plan, to create comprehensive policy whose legitimacy wins broad public support—in short, to "steer" under these conditions—requires the creation of an organized political will. The creation of such a will has proved difficult even in hard states with a clear sovereign authority; under the Madisonian Constitution, it promises to be a truly monumental task. Of course, yet another new frontier may be discovered somewhere in the near future, shifting the game back into a positive-sum mode; if so, the debate on the constitutional issue could be delayed indefinitely. All one can say is that, as of 1981, constraint seems to be moving in on America across the board.

But What Have You Done for Me Lately?

It is unlikely that any political system could survive very long if every possible interest became organized and moved into the political arena with the aim of realizing its specific objectives and blocking everyone else's. One of the most important tasks facing any ruling elite is to scale down demands on the political system to manageable proportions. This "mobilization of bias," as E. E. Schattschneider has called it,[24] is an essential ingredient of any political hegemony, contested or not. People may be born free and equal, but political interests are not. When mobilization of bias is made impossible by the entry of a wide range of new groups into the political arena, the system becomes overloaded. Not surprisingly, the overload problem has received a great deal of attention recently—not solely as an issue for the American polity but throughout the advanced industrial world. There are good reasons for this, as there are for supposing that overload represents a particularly serious problem for the American political system.

As was mentioned earlier, the ideal liberal capitalist state is grounded in rational instrumentality—for example, the limited-liability social compact among autonomous individuals, beloved of eighteenth-century political philosophers. The underlying rationale of the United States thus is quite different from those of older polities, and not necessarily legitimate in their eyes. The American emphasis on self-interest was an idea for which Edmund Burke sharply criticized the nascent political liberalism of his day.[25] This same issue was given much attention by Karl Marx and Frederick Engels in *The Communist Manifesto*; and it attracted the distinctly unfavorable notice of Pope Pius XI in the 1930s. Each in his own way, all these critics saw that the logic of capitalist social and political relations led toward each individual's *unlimited* pursuit of his own interests, dissolving all preceding collective and cooperative bonds among human beings and leaving nothing in the end but the "nexus of callous cash payment."[26] The capitalist philosophy was perceived as reducing all human relationships to exchange relationships, which means from either the old conservative or the socialist point of view

[24] *The Semi-Sovereign People* (New York: Holt, Rinehart, and Winston, 1960), pp. 20-61.

[25] "Society is indeed a contract. Subordinate contracts for objects of more occasional interest may be dissolved at pleasure; but the state ought not to be considered as nothing better than a partnership agreement in a trade of pepper and coffee, calico or tobacco, or some other such low concern, to be taken up for a little temporary interest, and to be dissolved by the fancy of the parties. It is to be looked on with other reverence." It is a partnership in all science, a partnership in every virtue and in all perfection. Edmund Burke, *Reflections on the Revolution in France*, in Ross J. Hoffman and Paul Levak, eds., *Burke's Politics* (New York: Alfred A. Knopf, 1949), p. 318.

[26] Karl Marx and Frederick Engels, *Selected Works* (Moscow: Foreign Languages Publishing House, 1962), p. 36.

that these relationships have become considerably less than fully human.

The United States, however, neither was intended to be nor became a *pure* capitalist society, defined *solely* in terms of self-interest and profitable exchange transactions. Such a society probably would be an unviable monstrosity. Something else is needed to create a functioning nation, something that produces bonds of sentiment which override citizens' pursuit of individual and group interests. As Joseph Schumpeter has suggested, one possibility is that traditional normative elements survive from precapitalist times into a capitalist era. Indeed, one of Schumpeter's chief concerns was that these older normative elements were evaporating in capitalist societies, and that traditional social and political relationships were disappearing with them.[27] Survival of traditional values was always a nonstarter in the United States, however, for reasons already discussed. What collective affective bonds held America together? The answer lies somewhere in the American consensus—and broadly, I believe, in an ideological cluster which could be called "republican virtue."[28] Louis Hartz to the contrary, more than John Locke's political and social joint-stock company was needed for the whole scheme to hang together, and it was this something more that republican virtue provided.

This cluster of interrelated ideas contained a number of components. Emotional identification with America as a *novus ordo seclorum*, a wholly new creation devoted to human liberty, was an essential ingredient. The nation's institutional symbols were the Declaration of Independence and the Constitution itself, rather than the dynastic trappings of earlier polities. Both documents very early became subjects of intense veneration in the American political culture. Young men proved amply in the Civil War and in both world wars that they were as ready to die for their object of collective affection as any other citizens were for theirs. This was all the more remarkable considering that in a real sense, the United States is a political abstraction compared with Europe; and it would be quite inexplicable if Americans were as exclusively oriented toward self-interest as the ideal capitalist man is supposed to be.

Republican virtue in the United States has always been closely linked with the pervasive importance of religion in American culture

[27] Joseph A. Schumpeter, *Capitalism, Socialism and Democracy*, 3d ed. (New York: 1950). Schumpeter observes, "The aristocratic element continued to rule the roost *right to the period of intact and vital capitalism*" (pp. 137-138).

[28] I am indebted to Professor Robert H. Salisbury of Washington University, St. Louis, for this term. He of course bears no responsibility whatever for what I have done with it here.

and social life. This link was by no means a necessary or self-evident component of the history of capitalism. Devotion to rationalism, science, technological innovation, and the pursuit of self-interest does not, after all, sit easily with traditional varieties of Judeo-Christian religion. America is anything but a logical society, however. The mainstream culture has typically supported free enterprise and religion together, denying as a matter of course the kind of tension between the two to which, for example, Pope Pius XI called attention in 1931.

In addition, economic ideology early took on a peculiar affective-bonding life of its own—which meant that it was doing its job of maintaining hegemony. The doctrine of the limited state was continually preached and largely accepted. Presidents Van Buren, Cleveland, and Hoover stated in virtually the same words: "It is the duty of the people to support the government, not of the government to support the people." So long as it was widely assumed that economic activity was in the private domain, two important results followed. First, the demands on government to ensure positive results with active public policy were limited. If most people did not expect such government activity, problems of overload could hardly arise. Second, to the extent that economic questions were not regarded as political, what happened in economics—short of catastrophic system-wide disaster—could not be attributed to anyone in particular, and least of all to specific political leaders. In such a setting, therefore, people were unlikely to develop the habit of making their support for the government contingent on its producing benefits for them in the here and now. Their fortunes were determined apart from the state and its leaders. The successes succeeded, the failures failed, and the middling sort remained in the middle: such was the nature of things, and such was the price of liberty.

American conservatives who feared the rise of the capitalist state in the 1930s often expressed deep concern that the government took on the job of supporting the people to some extent, the people would become dependent on the government and sink into a kind of Roman mob, kept quiet by bread and circuses. Such concern was natural enough, but it could be argued that the conservatives were looking for trouble in the wrong place. Politicized capitalism does not simply create dependency. By breaking down the isolative walls between the state on the one hand and the civil society and economy on the other, the capitalist state makes it increasingly evident that social and economic outcomes no longer arise out of the nature of things, but are consequences of political decisions. The state seeks social harmony. Once self-regulation among the citizenry breaks down, political action enters to replace it, to compensate for the breakdown and to overcome its more pathological effects. The choices politicians make in their quest for social harmony are responses to manifest pressure and demands, both general, as in a general crisis like the Great Depression, and particular. The more often the state intervenes—and especially the more often its interventions extend beyond the strictly economic sphere into relations among groups in society—the more obvious becomes its role in determining outcomes, and the more clamorous become the pressures that induce it to take that role.

A more or less inescapable paradox results. The state's efforts to ensure social harmony amount to efforts to maintain its general legitimacy. Recently, as the evolution of capitalism toward a high-technology basis has tended to eliminate many unskilled and semi-skilled jobs, the number of citizens who are economically helpless and dependent has expanded, and so have the state's compensatory interventions. Not only does the state's visibility in determining outcomes grow as it does this, but each new intervention is likely to establish a new program and a new relationship between an agency and a clientele group. If the interest group in question is of any political significance at all, the program, once embedded in the budget, acquires some of the attributes of immortality. The more the state's compensatory interventions spread, the more widely this lesson is learned. One consequence is that new organized interests proliferate in rough proportion to the success of earlier groups in getting a piece of the action. Another is a wave-like propagation of feelings on the part of those not yet effectively organized that government is illegitimately depriving them of a value it bestows on other people, very often their opponents in social or economic struggles. The ensuing politics of resentment has surfaced again and again in contemporary American elections, and in other ways as well, from the rise of George Wallace a decade ago to the current tax revolt. In short, the search for social harmony negates itself. The more the state pursues it, the more politicized the society becomes. The more politicized the society becomes, the greater the mobilization of interest groups, and the more widespread the questioning of the legitimacy of state actions. As this process unfolds, people's affective bonds to the state give way under the strain of proliferating demands.

It would be too much to say that politics in these circumstances comes increasingly to approach Hobbes's "war of all against all." Nevertheless, the old bonds of American patriotism, the limits on

99

citizens' demands imposed by older accepted doctrines of a limited state, and the moderating effect of republican virtue on unlimited pursuit of group interests all have been enormously corroded. No new political formula has come into existence that either legitimizes or regulates this politicized group struggle, and more seems immediately in prospect. It is hardly surprising that doctrines of laissez-faire have reemerged into so much popularity recently. Herbert Hoover and his compatriots in the 1930s may have been more right in their belief that the traditional constitution could not work or survive under political capitalism than most of their contemporaries thought. If so, however, it was not because the new active state produces a sodden mass of dependents, but because of the potentially infinite proliferation of interest groups and conflict among them. The concomitant decay of institutional channels and of diffuse affective support for the regime also has been a factor. Both of these developments have brought the political order closer and closer to the "pure" Madisonian fragmentation of power laid down in the Constitution on the one hand, and to the "pure" capitalist model of instrumental rationality and unlimited pursuit of self-interest on the other. This has led governability-crisis theorists such as Daniel Bell to call alarmed attention to the cultural contradictions of capitalism.[29] No state is likely to perform its essential functions very well if public attitudes to it change from veneration for the Constitution and the laws to that pure expression of political self-interest, "What have you done for me lately?" No society is likely to cohere with a purely hedonistic, individually self-aggrandizing public philosophy, since by definition this is no public philosophy. Yet we seem to be moving in this direction.

The Post-1960 "Revolution"

In the 1930s, the conservatives' critique of the new interventionist state seemed to most nonconservatives to be a parade of imaginary horribles. An important reason for this was that the New Deal represented only an early and quite limited variant of political capitalism. Many of the crucial precedents were set in the 1930s, to be sure; but the creature's bark at that point was far worse than its bite—as, for example, a review of the coverage and rates of the 1939 federal income tax should make clear. It is entirely characteristic of the New Deal's limited scope that from beginning to end many of its most characteristic social-welfare expenditures were classified in

[29] *The Cultural Contradictions of Capitalism* (New York: Basic Books, 1976).

the budget as "temporary-emergency" expenditures. It was widely expected that the New Deal's "alphabet soup" relief agencies would disappear when the economy entered boom again—and of course disappear they did after World War II came to the rescue.

As I have already pointed out, the decade from 1965 to 1975 was not only one of enormous proliferation in domestic programs and regulatory activity. It was also the period that contained the rise and fall of the Vietnam War; the disorganization of political parties; spectacular popular repudiations of presidents (Johnson, Nixon), followed by weak executives; a steep and apparently permanent decline in the public's trust and support for its rulers; a spate of power-dispersing reforms in national party conventions and the rules of the House of Representatives; an eruption of politically active single-interest groups; and a sharp decline in voting, particularly among those who already participated least to begin with. It would be difficult *not* to see the connections among these movements. They point directly at a rather extreme power vacuum, and at a new variant of pure Madisonian constitutional politics.

The new political capitalist state is not a passive government "at a distance and out of sight," however—quite the contrary. As conservatives never tire of complaining, it is very energetic and intrusive into areas of social and economic life that even in the New Deal era were entirely private. What happens when the state's active efforts to pursue social harmony and accumulate capital run up against its limits as a "Tudor polity"?

Imagine that the state confronts a need to respond to some dislocation in society and the economy, which has produced groups demanding government action in the streets, in the courts, or by lobbying. Each of the targets of this pressure responds in its own way. The state's response is therefore disaggregated: At every level, a different group of politicians is seeking to win votes and restore disturbed social harmony in its own area by creating a program and spending money. Each program requires the building of a bureaucratic agency—assume this takes place, finally, at the federal level. The new agency establishes close links with the clientele groups outside who are most directly interested in what it does, and with relevant key actors in the ultrafragmented American legislative process. A ratchet has been built into the system which, once created, will be most difficult to dissolve. Through the years the budget grows more and more uncontrollable because more and more such programs are locked in by congressional action, and only subsequent congressional action could unlock them.

James Madison at one point referred to the regime he had helped to create as "a feudal constitution."[30] At first glance this seems a curious description, in that the word *feudal* ordinarily applies to agriculturally based medieval European societies. Feudalism also has a purely structural connotation, however: It can be said to describe *any* arrangement that creates linkages of autonomous power which are only weakly connected to some central, nominally sovereign, authority. This is the sense in which Madison meant the term as he contemplated the ingenious political clockwork he and his colleagues had created in 1787. If he was correct, it may be that the American polity is even more extraordinarily ancient than Huntington thought.

As the pressures of the present push toward the creation of a hard state, they run up against this antique constitutional structure. What happens as a consequence? The structure does not become more consolidated; rather, its innately feudal character is strongly reinforced as political capitalism matures and develops. Countervailing forces—notably the traditional American parties—collapse under the strain of attempting to integrate a welter of mobilized single interests. A huge number of such interests now exist, for whom any effort at central coordination is anathema. They function as discrete molecules of political power, and they grow almost exponentially. The first and most important article of each of their creeds, however much they disagree otherwise, is that outsiders (presidents, parties, the public) should stay away from the turf they have staked out for themselves. The implications of this stance for the possibility of the state's acting to plan, control, and steer the polity in the *collective* national interest are profound. The strengthening of the feudal power structure probably has left us further from the development of a hard state based on democratic consent and public accountability than we were in 1960—or maybe even in 1865. Given the persistence of our liberal individualist cultural expectations, how can such feudalism possibly be made legitimate?

This dilemma may appear to be a clarion call for yet more big government, complete with big spending, big programs, and big

[30] "It may be said that the new Constitution is founded on different principles, and will have a different operation. I admit the difference to be material. It presents the aspect rather of a feudal system of republics, if such a phrase may be used, than of a Confederacy of independent states. And what has been the progress and event of the feudal Constitution? In all of them a continual struggle between the head and the inferior members, until a final victory has been gained in some instances by one, in others, by the other of them. . . . This form of Government, in order to effect its purposes must operate not within a small but an extensive sphere." Quoted in William Appleman Williams, *The Contours of American History* (Cleveland and New York: World, 1961), p. 149.

regulation. Anyone who understands the recent course of big public policy in the advanced industrial countries, however, is likely to be very skeptical of such a solution. In particular, large-scale bureaucracies set up for national economic planning and control have been inadequate wherever they have been created, from the ENI in Italy to NEDC (or "Neddy") in Britain to the Polish state as a whole. It seems quite a bit too late in the day for a simple-minded faith in the state as savior. The market's advantages as a mechanism for allocating resources strongly suggest that it should continue to play a significant role in the nation's economic and social life. Given that, why should we not simply return more closely to free-market economics, scaled-down political demand, and thereby a much closer fit between what capitalism requires and what the traditional constitutional order can provide? Many are asking this question these days, and answering that we should indeed.

The central issue, then, is not merely big government. Perhaps a more important point is that, ineffective as parliamentary democratic regimes may be at coping with the pressures of an adverse environment, the traditional constitutional structure of the United States may well be even more ineffective. On the international plane, these pressures include continuous rivalry among superpowers and critical-resource vulnerability; at home, the inability of capitalism to manage its affairs unaided or unsteered has drawn the state into intervening. Such an environment appears to call for a markedly higher degree of "stateness" at the political center than Americans have ever been used to apart from the temporary emergencies of wartime.

In this regard—and even granted the difficulties all advanced industrial polities are suffering from these days—no small part of the American regime's crisis seems to relate specifically to the number of discrete centers of power within the polity. Historically, feudal political structures are marked by the number and variety of people and institutions wielding governmental functions who are able to go into business for themselves. It is this propensity to go into business for oneself (and one's immediate clients and publics outside government) that is so conspicuous a feature of American government activity at present. The independence of these various power centers gives a cast of private enterprise—even at times laissez-faire private enterprise—to the activities of the state, of what the Romans called the public thing (res publica). Like all feudal structures, the one created by the American Constitution is immensely complicated. The complications overwhelm the capacity of any ordinary citizen to understand who or what is responsible for anything that happens.

Without working institutions—such as political parties—to bind together what the Founding Fathers so thoroughly separated, public confusion tends to become public revulsion and public apathy. Something of the sort has been going on over the past fifteen years or so.

Only an excessively short-sighted, parochial preoccupation with the interests of capitalism would find this development a matter of indifference, much less of celebration. The collective needs of those who control the means of production include a state that is *supported* by the public at large, not one that is merely tolerated or—worse still—held in contempt. This is true not only in the United States but in a wide range of situations—in Poland, for example, to take an extreme case. There, neither the official ideology nor the state's undisputed control of the means of force has been enough to create a minimum base of popular support for the regime—that is, those who directly control the so-called socialist mode of production. Support has to be *purchased*. Support also has to be purchased in the United States, although our problem is not outright revolt against an unpopular regime but widespread public cynicism, distrust, and apathy born of the confusion and paralysis created by the Madisonian power centrifuge.

To say that public support must continually be won anew, however, is not to imply that the state can do this by producing yet another program for each new interest group that develops the clout to make its way through the political labyrinth. Rather, if the state is to maintain its legitimacy within the democratic framework embedded in the Constitution, it must find a way to encourage citizens to create effective instruments of collective action. At the same time, the state needs to take on a reasonably clear political responsibility, shared by teams of politicians elected to be in charge of the steering mechanism. To put the matter slightly differently, part of the problem of big government in the United States arises from the power baronies that various interests have carved out as the state's attempts to act on behalf of the people have been thwarted by the fragmentation mandated by our "Tudor polity." This stalemate has created growing doubts among the public at large about the government's legitimacy. Indeed, it seems to have given political intervention a bad name, and thus has prompted a recurrent—and probably futile—search for a return to the "good old days" of laissez faire.

A good example of this problem is the businessman who complains bitterly about the burdens of time and energy that contemporary federal regulations impose on him. The main source of his frustration is the growing number of regulatory agencies to which, in one way or another, he is responsible in his record-keeping. This situation has arisen largely because Congress, operating in a completely disaggregated way, gives each agency it creates what amounts to a hunting license. It does so with little or no regard for the impact that other agencies and their hunting licenses already are having on the same individual or corporate subject of regulation. The resultant cry for deregulation and reliance on the market for mechanisms of allocation is a natural byproduct of this state of affairs, though in some industries, such reliance on the market would in fact produce serious and often unexpected social costs.

It is not impossible to imagine a situation in which regulation continued to exist because important public purposes required it, but in which it would be more rational and less burdensome. To accomplish this, however, would require a political structure that could offset the tendency of individual legislators, legislative committees, and agencies to run their own show, defend their own turf, and go into business for themselves with some concentration of internally sovereign power at the center of the state. The question of increasing or decreasing the public sector's control of private enterprise is secondary here—who would want to see *all* the walls of isolation created by the liberal capitalist state broken down? The fundamental issue is curbing what amounts to private enterprise within the state itself. Such restriction may well be required both to restore democratic popular support for the state, its decision makers, and its decisions, and to provide the relatively coherent steering capacity on which capitalism must rely in its present stage of the "governability-crisis, crisis-of-democracy" literature that has within the framework of the Tudor polity seems remote.

Considerations like these appear ultimately to be at the center of the "governability-crisis, crisis-of-democracy" literature that has flourished in the late 1970s. How can the state be given more power—and more autonomy from the demands of hyperpluralist politics—short of a turn to a permanent constitutional dictatorship vested in the chief executive? How can the needs of contemporary capitalism for a steering mechanism be reconciled with preserving the essential libertarian values for which the American republic has always stood? I have no magic formula to answer this question. Barring the unexpected creation of yet another frontier, however, we may expect that it will be asked more and more often as the United States moves—or drifts—toward the end of the twentieth century. Recognizing that a serious constitutional problem now exists is the first step toward raising this question, and hence toward publicly debating its implications.

5

The Constitution and
the Protection of Capitalism

Bernard H. Siegan

In my opinion, the U.S. Constitution provides for and secures a capitalist economy. The existence of capitalism requires that private enterprise and private markets be legally safeguarded and allowed to function freely. Government intervention in the economy is permissible, but only when very special circumstances demand it. Were it correctly interpreted, our present Constitution would accord sufficient protection for the commercial liberties—those relating to the ownership and use of property and to the freedom of contract to produce and distribute goods and services—to enable our economic system to function in a manner largely consistent with this description of capitalism.

The Constitution ratified in 1789 limited the economic powers of government and protected the exercise of the commercial liberties. These original safeguards were augmented with the adoption, first of the Fifth Amendment, and later of the Fourteenth. The course of events in contemporary times has not reduced the importance or desirability of preserving these liberties to warrant any departure from constitutional purpose in this area.

In this paper, I will first examine the intentions of constitutional framers with respect to these issues and will then turn to the contemporary scene to determine whether the framers' design is still appropriate in our day. The latter inquiry is directed at those who contend that the constitutional scheme may be modified when necessitated by contemporary experience.

Underlying this analysis is the assumption that a consensus exists among jurists and constitutional scholars that the intentions of constitutional framing bodies should be strictly observed when to do so would be advantageous or not harmful for modern society. Preservation of constitutional government requires at least this kind of commitment. In the absence of cause necessitating a different interpretation, there is no reason to depart from the terms and meanings of the fundamental law.

The position presented here is at variance with the construction given the Constitution by the contemporary Supreme Court. It is, however, similar to interpretations of earlier courts, particularly from 1897 to 1937, the period of economic due process. During that period, the high court examined federal and state laws dealing with social and economic matters, and declared many of them unconstitutional under either the Fifth or the Fourteenth Amendment because they deprived a complainant of property or liberty without due process of law. The contemporary Court, in contrast, usually upholds such legislation unless it violates certain specially protected liberties or is devoid of all rationality. Laws fixing prices, entry into markets, and output, or otherwise restricting production and distribution of goods and services, which could not have passed constitutional muster under the prior standard, have little difficulty surviving under the contemporary Court's rulings. Laws regulating the use and development of property are subject to somewhat greater scrutiny. Legislation restraining the exercise of what the contemporary Court considers fundamental liberties, on the other hand, such as freedom of speech, of the press, of religion, and of sexual privacy, receives much less deferential treatment. Any restriction in those areas is ordinarily set aside as unconstitutional unless the government can justify it as necessary to achieve a compelling state interest.

For the reasons to follow, I believe that this current judicial policy, which fails to secure the material liberties substantially, is contrary to the original purpose and intent of the Constitution and the form of capitalism it established.

The Ideas behind the Constitution

The Constitution was written at a time when ideas of natural law and the social compact were widely accepted and highly influential. Government was thought to be without authority to deprive people of their natural rights—those rights inherent in all people by virtue of their humanity. Among the most important of natural rights were those relating to ownership of property.

In reading accounts of the Constitutional Convention of 1787, one is impressed with the framers' dedication to securing legally the ownership of property. Thus, Gouverneur Morris, a prominent and influential delegate, asserted on the floor of the convention on July 5, 1787, "Life and liberty were generally said to be of more value, than property. An accurate view of the matter would nevertheless prove that property was the main object of Society."[1] Although probably not all fifty-five delegates to the convention shared Morris's views, it is apparent from the reports that the vast majority agreed that the preservation of property rights was a major objective of government. American and English political and intellectual leaders in the seventeenth and eighteenth centuries considered the right of property ownership to be a bulwark against authoritarianism. They valued this right as providing freedom, autonomy, and independence to the average citizen. For, they claimed, if the government could take away something owned by the individual, it could exert enormous power over the people. A person then would be reluctant to speak, write, pray, or petition in a manner displeasing to the authorities, lest he lose what he had already earned or legally acquired. Consequently, property was a foremost personal right, because the exercise of many other rights depended on it. The right of property meant that people could work, produce, invest, and create, secure in the knowledge that, except for taxes, they could retain the rewards of their labor and ingenuity. If government wanted to acquire their property, at least it would have to pay a fair price for it.

Most states at the time of the Constitutional Convention restricted voting to owners of real property. For many framers, a freeholder was the ideal voter. Frequently he was financially independent with a stake in the preservation of established society. To safeguard and encourage freeholding, a society must guarantee other liberties. For people to become freeholders required protection of their freedom to make contracts, for that is the only way to acquire property by one's own efforts. For freeholders to benefit from their property and remain independent of government also required protection of their freedom to contract to use and dispose of property.

The foremost authority on English law at the time of the Constitutional Convention was Sir William Blackstone. His four-volume *Commentaries on the Laws of England* is among the most influential legal works of all time. It is probable that the framers subscribed to Blackstone's definition that the right of private property is "absolute . . . [and] consists in the free use, enjoyment, and disposal [by man]

---

[1] Max Farrand, ed., *The Records of the Federal Convention of 1787*, 4 vols. (rev. ed., 1937; New Haven: Yale University Press, 1966), vol. 1, p. 533. See pp. 534 and 541-542 for similar expressions.

of all his acquisitions, without any control or diminution, save only by the laws of the land." This right was "probably founded in nature" but was subject to the state's powers of eminent domain (with full indemnification), of taxation (only by act of Parliament), and of regulation (gentle and moderate).[2]

It is well to consider some of Blackstone's positions in view of the great acceptance he had at the time of the Constitutional Convention. According to Blackstone, government was not entitled to acquire property from an owner without paying for it, no matter how meritorious the claim:

> So great moreover is the regard of the law for private property, that it will not authorize the least violation of it; no, not even for the general good of the whole community. If a new road, for instance, were to be made through the grounds of a private person, it might perhaps be extensively beneficial to the public; but the law permits no man, or set of men, to do this without consent of the owner of the land. In vain may it be urged, that the good of the individual ought to yield to that of the community; for it would be dangerous to allow any private man or even any public tribunal to be the judge of this common good, and to decide whether it be expedient or no. Besides, the public good is in nothing more essentially interested, than in the protection of every individual's private rights, as modelled by the municipal law. In this and similar cases, the legislature alone can and frequently does, interpose, and compel the individual to acquiesce. But how does it interpose and compel? Not by absolutely stripping the subject of his property in an arbitrary manner; but by giving him a full indemnification and equivalent for the injury thereby sustained. The public is now considered as an individual, treating with an individual for an exchange. All that the legislature does is to oblige the owner to alienate his possessions for a reasonable price; and even this is an exertion of power, which the legislature indulges with caution, and which nothing but the legislature can perform.[3]

Rejecting retrospective laws, Blackstone wrote that all laws should be made to commence in futuro, so that everyone would be aware of them before committing to action.[4] Such a rule prohibits denial of an

---

[2] William Blackstone, *Commentaries on the Laws of England*, 4 vols. (Oxford, 1765-1769), vol. 1, pp. 134, 135, 140.

[3] Ibid., p. 135.

[4] Ibid., p. 46.

existing property or economic interest and thus prevents the imposition of many government controls over commerce. Laws imposing excessive restraint, moreover, were arbitrary and oppressive:

> [Civil liberty] is no other than natural liberty so far restrained by human laws (and no further) as is necessary and expedient for the general advantage of the public. Hence we may collect that the law, which restrains a man from doing mischief to his fellow citizens, though it diminished the natural, increases the civil liberty of mankind: but every wanton and causeless restraint of the will of the subject, whether practiced by a monarch, a nobility, or a popular assembly, is a degree of tyranny. Nay, that even laws themselves, whether made with or without our consent, if they regulate and constrain our conduct in matters of mere indifference, without any good end in view, are laws destructive of liberty. . . . [T]hat constitution or frame of government, that system of laws, is alone calculated to maintain civil liberty, which leaves the subject entire master of his own conduct, except in those points wherein the public good requires some direction or restraint.[5]

Under the common-law rules as enunciated by Blackstone, government could not confiscate or arbitrarily regulate the use and enjoyment of property. Within these limits, government could set rules to resolve conflicts among those having or affected by interests in property. A private market cannot exist in the absence of laws and covenants that define or create the rights of ownership or other interests in property. Most important, however, the limitation on government powers as described by Blackstone shielded investment expectations and enabled a private market to function. Under it, investors were relatively secure against oppressive political conduct. The common-law protection against confiscation later became the "taking" clause in the Fifth Amendment, which provides that "private property shall not be taken for public use without just compensation."

Restraints on Commercial Powers of the States

The Constitutional Convention treated the commercial powers of the federal and state governments differently. A major purpose for establishing the union was to limit the authority of the states in commercial matters. James Madison, Alexander Hamilton, and John Marshall, among others, advise us that violations of economic liberties

[5] Ibid., pp. 121-122.

in the states were a principal reason behind the calling of the convention.[6] Concern over this problem is evident in the Constitution. Article I, section 10 prohibits the states from emitting bills of credit, from creating their own currency, from passing ex post facto laws or laws impairing the obligation of contracts, and from levying imposts or duties on imports or exports without the consent of Congress. The power given Congress in Article I, section 8 to regulate commerce "among the several states" further diminishes the states' powers over interstate commerce. Most important of the foregoing provisions in furthering a private market are the ex post facto and obligation of contracts clauses. Article I, section 9 also contains an ex post facto clause, one that applies to the federal government.

As now interpreted, the ex post facto clauses ban only retroactive penal and not civil laws. Yet at the time the Constitution was drafted and ratified, many if not most lawyers and lay people referred to all retroactive laws as ex post facto. In 1798, the U.S. Supreme Court, in *Calder* v. *Bull*, limited the application of these clauses to criminal matters.[7] Although it remains the law, this opinion has been the subject of much controversy ever since. Some eminent early jurists (Justices Joseph Story and William Johnson, and Chancellor James Kent) and many leading commentators over the years have contended that legislative deprivations of property rights were also forbidden by the ex post facto clauses. Under the broad definition, an ex post facto law is one that changes an existing law to the detriment of the person who has acted in reliance on it. Had the broad definition prevailed, the impact on the nation's domestic policy would be substantial. A broadly defined ex post facto clause would prevent government from denying or removing property or other economic interests that were lawfully acquired.

According to John Marshall, in the only dissent he wrote in a constitutional matter during his thirty-four years as chief justice of the U.S. Supreme Court, the contracts clause was intended to protect the freedom to enter into and make contracts from molestation by the states. The case in question was *Ogden* v. *Saunders* (1827), and the issue was whether a New York bankruptcy law enacted prior to the execution of a promissory note could affect the obligation between

---

[6] *Letters and Other Writings of James Madison,* 4 vols. (Philadelphia: J. B. Lippincott, 1865), vol. 1, p. 350; *The Papers of Alexander Hamilton,* ed. Harold C. Syrett and others, 26 vols. (New York: Columbia University Press, 1961-1979), vol. 25, p. 479; Ogden v. Saunders, 25 U.S. (12 Wheat.), pp. 354-355 (1837) (Marshall, Chief Justice, dissenting).

[7] 3 U.S. (3 Dall.) 386 (1798).

the parties to that note.[8] For Justice Marshall, the only binding provisions in legitimate contracts were those that the parties themselves chose to incorporate. Laws that altered these provisions, whether passed before or after the execution of a contract, impaired the contractual obligations of the parties. The case was decided on a 4–3 vote, largely because the four justices in the majority sought to uphold the power of the states to pass bankruptcy laws, a power that Marshall's dissent would have effectively denied. At that time, no bankruptcy law existed at the federal level. Had Marshall prevailed, the regulatory powers of the states would have been severely limited. Accordingly, much existing state economic regulation would not be constitutional if either the ex post facto or obligations of contracts clause were broadly interpreted, as some leading authorities contend they should have been.

Even in the absence of specific constitutional protection, early justices applied natural law theory to protect property interests from infringement by the states. Since these justices were mostly of Federalist persuasion, it may reasonably be assumed that the position they took in these cases reflected views dominant at the Constitutional Convention. In *Fletcher* v. *Peck* (1810), per Chief Justice Marshall, and *Terrett* v. *Taylor* (1815), per Justice Story, the Supreme Court struck down legislation in whole or in part on the basis that the nature of government restrained the legislative power over private property even where federal or state constitutions are silent in the matter.[9] In these cases, the state legislatures had enacted legislation divesting owners of property that they had acquired in good faith.

Commercial Liberties at the Federal Level

The framers' intentions regarding protection of property and economic liberties are not as clear at the federal level as they are with respect to the states, although they are clearly inclined in the same direction. The contracts clause does not affect the federal government, but the ex post facto clauses, were they broadly interpreted, would cover much of the same area. Complicating the analysis is that for some leaders, such as Madison, Hamilton, and Marshall, lodging powers in the national government was a means of preserving liberty.[10] They

[8] 25 U.S. (12 Wheat.) 212 (1827).

[9] 10 U.S. (6 Cranch.) 87 (1810); 13 U.S. (9 Cranch.) 43 (1815).

[10] See *The Federalist*, no. 10 (Madison), no. 7 (Hamilton); Albert Beveridge, *The Life of John Marshall*, 4 vols. (Boston and New York: Houghton, Mifflin, 1916), vol. 1, pp. 223-232, 416-417; see also works cited in note 6.

feared that for those powers to be left in the hands of state authorities would result in greater limitations on personal freedoms.

During the Constitutional Convention, the framers rejected granting significant economic powers to the federal government. They refused to empower the national government to grant charters of incorporation; to establish seminaries for the promotion of literature and the arts; to establish public institutions, rewards, and immunities for the promotion of agriculture, commerce, trades, and manufactures; to regulate stages on the post roads; to establish a university; to encourage, by proper premiums and provisions, the advancement of useful knowledge and discoveries; to open or establish canals; to emit bills on the credit of the United States (which would include notes for circulation as currency); and to make sumptuary laws.[11] Each of these powers was proposed and either voted down or not considered further outside of committee. The accounts also suggest that delegates may have rejected other efforts to empower Congress to grant monopolies except for patents and copyrights.[12]

It may be, as some contend, that almost all the foregoing powers were meant to be included in the power over commerce or in other powers given to Congress. As of September 14, 1787, three working days before final adjournment, and after the language relating to commerce and other major national powers had been settled, some influential and prominent delegates apparently believed either that the convention did not confer extensive economic powers on the federal government or that the constitutional language on this point was not clear. On that day, Benjamin Franklin moved to add to Article I, section 8, after the language giving Congress power to establish post offices and post roads, "a power to provide for cutting canals where deemed necessary." James Madison moved to enlarge the motion "to grant charters of incorporation when the interests of the U.S. might require and legislative provisions of individual states may be incompetent." James Wilson, who later became a Supreme Court justice, seconded Franklin's motion, and Edmund Randolph, who later became the first U.S. attorney general, seconded Madison's. Such powers would appear to be inherent in a government possessed of substantial authority, and if this were the case there was no need to authorize them specifically. Franklin's motion was rejected by a vote of eight states to three, and Madison noted, "The other part fell of course, as including the power rejected."[13]

[11] Farrand, *Records*, vol. 2, pp. 303-304, 308-311, 321-326, 344, 351, 611, 615-616, 620.
[12] Ibid., vol. 3, pp. 375-376.
[13] Ibid., vol. 2, pp. 615-616, 611, 620.

We cannot be certain, of course, why these proposals were voted down. However, the episode does lend credence to the position that the Constitution did not grant Congress very extensive economic powers. In opposing legislation before the House of Representatives in 1791, to authorize a national bank, Madison (a member of the House) argued that the measure was unconstitutional, citing (among other things) the convention's rejection of federal chartering of corporations.[14] Years later, Madison explained that the proposal on canals had been rejected as conveying a power either improper to be invested in Congress or not likely to be yielded by the states.[15]

Consistent with what seems to have been his position during the convention, Madison, in *The Federalist*, minimized the scope of the congressional power to "regulate Commerce . . . among the several states" (Article I, section 8, clause 3). The commerce clause, which also allows regulation of trade with foreign nations and Indian tribes, is one, he asserted, "which few opposed and from which no apprehensions are entertained."[16] This clause was not an important issue in the ratification debates and met with only scattered opposition, the domestic portion apparently not being thought of as a grant of extensive power to the national government. Hamilton did not expound on the domestic power in *The Federalist*. Madison maintained his interpretation of the commerce clause through the years. In 1829, he stated that the federal government's power over domestic commerce was not intended to be as extensive as that over foreign commerce; the former was negative and meant to prevent injustice among the states rather than intended for the positive purposes of the federal government.[17]

To be sure, many dispute Madison's assessment. Even if he were incorrect, however, and the framers intended to grant a large commercial power to the national government, it is doubtful that their purpose was to increase economic regulation. Believing that economic liberties were more secure under federal than state authorities, they sought to preempt state economic controls. They inserted the contracts clause and other restraints to prevent economic abuses by the states. The commerce clause was similarly inspired.

Madison asserted in his famous *Federalist* number 10 that a "rage for paper money, for an abolition of debts, for an equal division of property, or any other improper or wicked project, will be less apt

14 Ibid., vol. 3, p. 362; for other views of this issue, see ibid., pp. 363, 375-376.
15 Ibid., pp. 463, 494-495.
16 *The Federalist*, no. 45 (Madison).
17 Farrand, *Records*, vol. 3, 478.

to pervade the whole body of the Union than any particular member of it."[18] He echoed the views of prominent nationalists such as Hamilton and Marshall who wanted to confine governmental authority over people. Thus, Howard Mann concludes that decisions of the Marshall Court supporting a broad interstate commerce power nationalized private rights and personal liberties to secure them against arbitrary state interference.[19]

The framers may not have sought to impose a rigid laissez-faire program, for as we know, Hamilton (as first secretary of the Treasury) and the Federalist-dominated first Congress favored some mercantilist policies. They did believe, however, that individual liberties, private property, and private enterprise were safer under federal auspices. Under this interpretation, the domestic commerce clause, a major ground for the proliferation of national economic controls over the years, was originally intended to accomplish just the reverse: to curb government regulation.

The Fourteenth Amendment

Measured by frequency of invocation, no provision in the Constitution is more important than the Fourteenth Amendment. Prior to the ratification of this amendment, the Bill of Rights was interpreted as affecting only laws passed by the federal government and not the states. Passage of the amendment enabled the Supreme Court to apply to the states, case by case, various provisions in the Bill of Rights. The Court has by now ruled that most, but not all, of the first eight amendments affect the states.

Congress framed the Fourteenth Amendment in 1866, primarily to guarantee and constitutionalize the Civil Rights Act of that year which gave blacks the same civil rights as whites and provided for federal enforcement of these rights. The amendment was ratified by the states two years later. The famous language of the last sentence of section 1 describes what was to be safeguarded:

> No State shall make or enforce any law which shall abridge the privileges or immunities of citizens of the United States; nor shall any State deprive any person of life, liberty or property without due process of law; nor deny to any person within its jurisdiction the equal protection of the law.

[18] *The Federalist,* no. 10 (Madison).
[19] H. Howard Mann, "The Marshall Court: Nationalization of Private Rights and Personal Liberty from the Authority of the Commercial Clause," *Indiana Law Review,* vol. 38 (1963), p. 117.

It is generally agreed that these three clauses secured more than merely the objectives of the Civil Rights Act of 1866; but the precise extent of the protections they established is not clear from the records of either Congress or the ratifying conventions. Among the priorities of the framers, however, protecting property and economic liberties rated high. Both can be considered "privileges or immunities of citizens of the United States," as those terms had been previously defined, and property ownership can be regarded as an interest protected under the due process clause, in accordance with prior interpretations of the U.S. and New York supreme courts.

In the opinion of four justices of the Supreme Court that considered the first major test of section 1, the Fourteenth Amendment provided extensive protection for economic liberties. These four were the dissenters in the *Slaughter-House Cases* decided in 1872.[20] In 1869, Louisiana's legislature granted a twenty-five year exclusive privilege to a private corporation it had created to operate a regulated livestock and slaughterhouse business within a specified area of about 1150 square miles, comprising New Orleans and two other parishes. This law required that all cattle brought into this area for commercial purposes be slaughtered by the corporation or in its facilities. An association of butchers adversely affected brought suit on the basis that the monopoly grant violated the Thirteenth and Fourteenth amendments. The Supreme Court held by a 5–4 vote that the monopoly grant was not invalid under the new amendments. The dissenters contended that despite the seeming remoteness of the facts to the purposes of the Fourteenth Amendment, the Louisiana statute violated one or more of the last three clauses of section 1.

In its opinion, the majority reduced the meaning of the privileges and immunities clause to make it a relatively insignificant provision, a condition from which it has never recovered. In subsequent years, however, the Court overturned a major holding of the *Slaughter-House Cases* by gradually expending the coverage of the due process clause to include, by unanimous decision in 1897, the liberty of contract to produce and distribute goods and services.[21] The due process clause likewise provided strong protection for property ownership until 1926, when the Court declared zoning to be constitutional, substantially reducing the previously operative guarantees. In a 1937 decision, the Court terminated economic due process and thereby the consider-

[20] 83 U.S. (16 Wall.) 36 (1872).
[21] Allgeyer v. Louisiana, 165 U.S. 578 (1897).

able protection previously afforded economic liberties.[22] During the economic due process period (1897–1937), the Court had in effect reversed the *Calder* (ex post facto) and *Ogden* (obligation of contracts) decisions.

In expanding the due process clause to include liberty of contract, the Supreme Court was invoking the historical understanding that adherence to due process requires government to rule by laws which do not arbitrarily deprive people of their liberties. Under our constitutional system, the judiciary has the responsibility for making determinations of this nature. The high court found that in the absence of strong justification or special circumstances, denial of an economic liberty violated due process of law.

The majority opinion in the *Slaughter-House Cases* considered the equal protection clause as confined to racial relations. The opinion expressed doubt that any other concern would ever come within the purview of this provision. This prediction has not been borne out, of course. Through the years, the clause has been applied to a variety of matters unrelated to race. The Warren Court introduced an egalitarian aspect to it that some commentators thought (or hoped) made it a monitor of economic equality in the society. They referred to it as the "new equal protection."

This egalitarian perspective has no basis in the origin of the clause, however. There is no evidence that during the debates over its framing and ratification, any significant group of officials or citizens wanted the Fourteenth Amendment to serve as an economic leveler. Even members of the antislavery movement, who were among those desiring the broadest coverage for the amendment, sought protection against state government, not benevolence from it. They wanted the Fourteenth Amendment to be a sweeping guarantee by the federal government of free exercise of political, material, and intellectual rights within the states. Among the rights given prime attention by the abolitionists were those of property and contract. They urged that these liberties be extended to all people, for these rights would give the poor the chance to become financially secure and independent.[23]

The original goals of the Fourteenth Amendment thus conflict with later egalitarian notions that the states should engage in law-

---

[22] Village of Euclid v. Ambler Realty Co., 272 U.S. 365 (1926) (zoning); West Coast Hotel v. Parrish, 300 U.S. 379 (1937) (economic due process).

[23] See William E. Nelson, "The Impact of the Antislavery Movement upon Styles of Judicial Reasoning in Nineteenth Century America," *Harvard Law Review*, vol. 87 (1974), pp. 513, 552.

making to reduce economic inequalities. These goals are evident in the language of the equal protection clause, which like that of the two prior clauses, is directed at eliminating laws that deprive people of their rights. When the equal protection clause is given a leveling interpretation, it no longer operates to reduce state action but instead allows or mandates more state legislation to accomplish particular objectives.

"Equal protection of the law" meant the equality of all people under human laws; blacks were to have the same civil rights as whites. Congress and the Court could nullify state laws that denied blacks the legal protections that whites enjoyed. Blacks would then have the same legal opportunities as whites to elevate their economic condition. The Supreme Court held in 1883 that the Fourteenth Amendment did not empower Congress to make racial discrimination in public accommodations unlawful. In striking down the Civil Rights Act of 1875, the Court said that the amendment did not authorize Congress to adjust the social rights of men and races in the community, but merely to provide "modes of redress against the operation of state laws . . . when these are subversive of the fundamental rights specified in the amendment." The Court concluded that the "abrogation and denial of rights, for which the states alone were, or could be responsible, was the great seminal and fundamental wrong which was intended to be remedied."[24] Accordingly, contemporary jurisprudence that incorporates notions of equality of condition into the equal protection clause renders it conceptually antagonistic to the other two clauses and makes the amendment incoherent.

Costs and Consequences of Economic Regulation

By its language and intent, then, the U.S. Constitution limits federal and state regulation of economic activity. This interpretation was accepted by the Supreme Court during the first third of this century, during the period of economic due process. A majority of the justices in those years required government to show strong justification for regulation before they would sustain it. The Court struck down many economic restraints, and this policy inhibited the federal, state, and local governments from imposing others. A principal reason for the reversal of this policy in 1937 was the belief that it did not serve the pragmatic interests of society. A new majority emerged of justices who believed that society generally benefited from economic regulatory legislation and that consequently the prior policy was not in the nation's best interest. This change in position occurred at a time

[24] Civil Rights Cases, 109 U.S. 3 (1883).

when economic regulation was still in its infancy in this country, and not much was understood about its cost and consequences—a void that has since been amply filled. We now have a large amount of economic regulation, and our comprehension of it is much greater.

In recent years, numerous studies have been made of regulation and regulatory agencies, measuring and evaluating their costs and benefits. Economic regulation—that is, government controls over the use and development of property and of the production and distribution of goods and services—appears to emanate chiefly from two different sources. The first source is those people who demand the passage of laws to remedy what they see as problems in the economic system. They may be motivated by ideological or more general public interest reasons. Members of this group do not directly benefit from the laws they propose or favor. The second source is those individuals and corporations who seek regulation in their own self-interest. Most of the people in this group are in business, trades, or professions. They want to limit competition or impose other restraints, usually as a means of obtaining more income for themselves.

The second group accounts for a great deal of regulation—perhaps most of it. Given a system that is highly receptive to economic regulation, relatively small numbers of persons seeking to obtain monetary gains have considerable opportunity to do so. Richard Posner has suggested that the lawmaking process creates a market for legislation in which politicians "sell" legislative protection to those who can help their electoral prospects with money or votes or both.[25] Michael Granfield has likened the legislature to a general store whose inventory includes monopolies, preferences, and concessions. The politician sells these goods, as any astute storeowner would, to the group offering the highest price. This arrangement does not necessarily include bribery or any other illegal activity; it may simply involve a legal contribution or a promise of votes.[26]

The process that leads to legislation benefiting comparatively few people is not difficult to understand. Those who would be helped substantially by laws have the incentive to wage a strong lobbying effort, whereas those who would bear the costs without sharing the benefits frequently do not have sufficient personal stake to fight for their position. The concentration of benefits provides the interest group in question with an incentive for creating a narrow political

[25] Richard Posner, *Economic Analysis of Law*, 2d ed. (Boston: Little, Brown and Co., 1977), p. 405.

[26] Michael Granfield, "Concentrated Industries and Economic Performance," *Large Corporations in a Changing Society*, ed. J. Fred Weston (New York: New York University Press, 1975), p. 164.

lobby, whose small size makes organizing relatively easy. On the other side, a larger number of citizens are involved; they are often widely dispersed and frequently have little or no knowledge of the proposed laws or their probable effects. Further, the costs of the legislation are spread so that few persons suffer very much, which limits incentive to organize. As a result, the costs of spending measures, subsidies, and special economic preferences are passed along, often to an unknowing and uncomplaining public. In this environment, the well-being of politically powerless property owners and entrepreneurs can be precarious. Reform groups who reject or distrust market mechanisms, and business interests who seek to eliminate competition, have considerable opportunity to achieve their goals, particularly when they have common aims, as they often do.

Special economic interest groups have been highly successful in their legislative efforts since the demise of economic due process. This is evident from the many instances in which the Supreme Court has sustained regulation that benefits special interests. Looking at these cases reveals much about the character and extent of regulation for which such groups have been responsible. An excellent illustration is the case of *Minnesota* v. *Clover Leaf Creamery Co.*, decided by the U.S. Supreme Court in January 1981.[27]

In 1977, Minnesota enacted a law banning the retail sale of milk in plastic, nonreturnable, nonrefillable containers, but permitting sale in other nonreturnable, nonrefillable containers, such as paperboard milk cartons. Milk sellers and others involved in producing and distributing plastic milk containers filed suit in a Minnesota state court, complaining that the statute deprived them of their right to engage in a legitimate enterprise and served no other purpose than unjustly enriching others in the same business.

The Minnesota trial court agreed; it found that, contrary to advancing certain alleged purposes—promoting conservation of resources, easing solid waste disposal problems, and conserving energy—the "actual basis" for the act "was to promote the economic interests of certain segments of the local dairy and pulpwood industry at the expense of the economic interests of other segments of the dairy industry and the plastics industry." The law did little to further the public interest; therefore there was no justification for the serious financial harm it caused many entrepreneurs and investors. The court declared the law unconstitutional under the due process clause of the Fourteenth Amendment, and its ruling was upheld by the Minnesota Supreme Court. The state appealed this interpretation of federal law

[27] 101 S. Ct. 715 (1981).

to the U.S. Supreme Court, which reversed the Minnesota courts and sustained the statute. The high court applied its policy of upholding economic regulation if there is any conceivable basis for the law or unless it violates one of the Court's preferred liberties.

Considerations similar to those that caused the Minnesota legislature to pass the plastic container law were probably involved in the passage of a host of other economic regulations upheld by the Supreme Court through the years. The Court has sustained a congressional ban on the interstate shipment of filled milk (a blend of skimmed milk and a fat or oil), a Kansas statute that threw debt adjustors who were not lawyers out of business, a New Orleans ordinance outlawing the peddling of foodstuffs in the French Quarter by a person licensed and engaged in the business, an Oklahoma law forbidding opticians to fit old eyeglasses to new frames without a prescription signed by an optometrist or opthalmologist and also prohibiting department stores from renting space to optometrists, a North Dakota law barring chain drugstores from the state, a Maryland law requiring oil companies to divest themselves of retail service stations, and a California law requiring permission from the state's new motor vehicle board to establish an automobile dealership.[28] It is not necessary to do a cost-benefit analysis to conclude that these laws benefit little more of the public than those who lobbied for them and were otherwise responsible for their passage. All these laws deprive individuals or corporations of their liberty to engage in legitimate economic activities. They harm society by limiting the production and distribution of goods and services, curtailing competition, and raising prices. They constitute unnecessary regulation, benefiting only the special interests of small groups. Were curbs on freedom of expression, religion, or sexual privacy involved, the Supreme Court would readily terminate them.

A large number of state occupational licensing laws can be similarly criticized. The practice of licensing those who want to engage in certain occupations is widespread in the nation. In 1969, according to Walter Gellhorn, a leading commentator in the field, California, the most restrictive of the states in this respect, required licenses for the practice of 178 occupations. Pennsylvania came next, with 165. The least restrictive state was West Virginia, which licensed

---

[28] United States v. Carolene Products Co., 304 U.S. 144 (1938); Ferguson v. Skrupa, 372 U.S. 726 (1963); City of New Orleans v. Dukes, 427 U.S. 297 (1976); Williamson v. Lee Optical Co., 348 U.S. 483 (1955); North Dakota State Board of Pharmacy v. Snyder's Drug Stores, Inc., 414 U.S. 156 (1973); Exxon Corporation v. Governor of Maryland, 437 U.S. 117 (1978); and New Motor Vehicle Board v. Orrin W. Fox Co., 439 U.S. 96 (1978).

63 occupations.[29] Occupational licensing is invariably justified as a means of protecting the public against unscrupulous and incompetent practitioners. Gellhorn suggests, however, that a much greater number of honest and able individuals are being excluded from their preferred work. He states that restricting entry is the real purpose and not merely a side effect of many if not most successful campaigns to institute licensing schemes:

> Licensing, imposed ostensibly to protect the public, almost always impedes only those who desire to enter the occupation or "profession"; those already in practice remain entrenched without a demonstration of fitness or probity. The self-interested proponents of a new licensing law generally constitute a more effective political force than the citizens who, if aware of the matter at all, have no special interest which moves them to organize in opposition. . . . The restrictive consequence of licensure is achieved in large part by making entry into the regulated occupation expensive in time or money or both.[30]

Gellhorn sums up the objections to these practices as follows:

> Occupational licensing has typically brought higher status for the producer of services at the price of higher costs to the consumer; it has reduced competition; it has narrowed opportunity for aspiring youth by increasing the costs of entry into a desired occupational career; it has artificially segmented skills so that needed services, like health care, are increasingly difficult to supply economically; it has fostered the cynical view that unethical practices will prevail unless those entrenched in a profession are assured of high incomes; and it has caused a proliferation of official administrative bodies, most of them staffed by persons drawn from and devoted to furthering the interest of the licensed occupations themselves.[31]

Nor do cost-benefit studies show that the public fares much better from economic regulation sponsored or advanced by public interest groups. Frequently, of course, it is difficult to determine who or what was actually responsible for passing the regulation. Thus, persuasive evidence exists that railroad regulation in the late nineteenth century did not come about, as some historians assert, because of public out-

[29] Walter Gellhorn, "The Abuse of Occupational Licensing," *University of Chicago Law Review*, vol. 44 (1976), p. 6.

[30] Ibid., pp. 11-12.

[31] Ibid., pp. 16-18.

rage at the "robber barons." Actually, most railroads supported regulation in 1887, when Congress created the Interstate Commerce Committee. They believed regulation would help them impose an industrywide cartel, something they had been unable to accomplish by themselves—nor were they wrong.

In my book *Economic Liberties and the Constitution*, I have summarized fifty-three studies of regulation, by more than sixty individual and institutional researchers, which have appeared in the scholarly literature.[32] These studies cover transportation, electric utilities, natural gas, banking, securities, broadcasting, foods and beverages, zoning, pharmaceuticals, insurance, agriculture, and eyeglass advertising. The vast bulk of these reports favor either total or substantial deregulation of the area under study. Although this compilation is not necessarily representative of existing learned opinion on regulation, both the number of areas covered and the amount of research involved is sufficiently large and varied to warrant serious consideration of the conclusions presented. I believe that a representative sampling of the scholarly literature would not yield an appreciable difference in opinion about the consequences of regulation. These studies show that although every regulation accomplishes some purpose, a vast number fail a cost-benefit analysis—that is, overall, the disadvantages outweigh the advantages. Much regulation has resulted in a reduction of economic efficiency, misallocation of resources, and a redistribution of income from the consumer to the regulated group. A common finding in these studies is that regulation raises prices, first, by restricting the market from competition, and second, by imposing a variety of requirements on producers and sellers that increase costs. People of average and lesser income, those least able to afford higher prices, are the most adversely affected. This wide consensus should dispel any doubt that the problem lies with regulation itself and not with those who administer it. Highlights of some of these studies follow:

Airlines. A study by Theodore E. Keeler, the 1975 report of the Subcommittee on Administrative Practice and Procedure of the Senate Judiciary Committee, and the 1975 report of the Civil Aeronautics Board Special Staff conclude that regulation substantially raises prices and distorts competition and efficiency. A study by the U.S. General Accounting Office asserts that without federal regulation of airlines during the six-year period 1969–1974, fares would been 22–55 percent less. The lower fares would have saved domestic air passengers between $1.4 billion and $1.8 billion a year.

---

[32] Bernard H. Siegan, *Economic Liberties and the Constitution* (Chicago: University of Chicago Press, 1980).

Trucking. Thomas Gale Moore has reported on the price effect of trucking regulations. In 1950, some products that previously had been transported only by regulated carriers were declared by the courts to be exempt from regulation by the Interstate Commerce Commission. As a result of these decisions, transportation prices declined substantially—about 12–59 percent in particular markets, with an unweighted average of 33 percent for fresh poultry and 36 percent for frozen, and a weighted average decline for frozen fruit and vegetables of 19 percent. Member firms of the National Broiler Council ship fresh poultry by exempt carriers and cooked poultry by regulated carriers. In surveying rates for the same routes between the same points, the council found that average unregulated rates were 33 percent lower than regulated ones. Comparisons of trucking rates between countries show that rates in nations with little or no regulation were 43 percent lower than rates in West Germany (which has strict controls) and the United States. Moore concludes that three-quarters of the cost of trucking regulations to shippers, and ultimately to consumers, takes the form of income transfers to labor and capital engaged in that industry.

Milk. Reuben A. Kessel has discussed the federal regulation of milk prices in 1967, under which about 60 percent of all milk shipped from farms passed through bottlers or dairies whose prices and other marketing practices were regulated. The regulations in effect permitted milk producers to exercise control over the dairies. Kessel found that regulated producers benefited but unregulated producers did not. The legislation favors the suppliers of fluid milk products and injures suppliers of milk for manufacturing. It thus increases the price of a necessity, milk, and lowers the prices of luxuries, ice cream, for example. By raising the price of milk, the regulation encourages too much production, so that resources are not being used most efficiently. The regulation also decreases competition and efficiency in the industry. Kessel concludes that the gains to some classes are outweighed by the losses to others and that therefore the regulation results in a net loss.

Zoning. My study of Houston, Texas, the nation's fifth largest city and the only major one that has never adopted zoning, indicates that its market system has made land use more responsible to consumer demand than it generally is with zoning. I compared prices of single-family houses and rents for multi-family dwellings in the Houston standard metropolitan statistical area (SMSA) with prices and rents in zoned areas, principally the Dallas SMSA. For the period studied, the absence of zoning did not appreciably affect prices of single-family homes, but it did cause rents to be lower. The pattern of land use in Houston is probably not appreciably different from what it would have been under zoning.

Lynne B. Sagalyn and George Sternlieb studied certain zoning and building requirements in New Jersey. They concluded that reducing three major zoning requirements—lot size, lot frontage, and living area—would reduce prices considerably and enlarge the effective housing market, provided that builders made a concomitant change in design of the housing they offered—an action that they probably would take. Changing two building code specifications—thickness of exterior wall sheeting and size of foundation cinder block—would also lower selling prices, but not to the same degree as altering zoning policies.

Liability insurance. Paul L. Joskow has examined state rate-making and risk-classification regulations in the property liability insurance industry and found that regulations restrict competition and increase prices. In addition, they cause an expansion of capacity beyond the efficient level. Joskow further concludes that the basis for the regulation is faulty. Using as an example California, which since 1947 has employed minimal regulation of the industry, he shows that relatively open competition has had excellent results. California premiums are lower, and no mass bankruptcies or price wars have occurred. Although supply shortages exist, they are less severe than in other states. The study recommends movement away from rate regulation and cartel pricing to open competition as a means of eliminating performance problems in the industry.

Agricultural price supports. Clay L. Cochran has surveyed agricultural price-support regulations—those intended to increase the incomes of rural people—and concludes that the regulations have not fulfilled their purpose. Only the incomes of the largest producers have increased significantly, while smaller producers have hardly benefited.

Eyeglass advertising. Lee Benham has examined restrictions on advertising in the eyeglass industry. In 1963, the year under study, approximately three-quarters of the states had some regulation against advertising. Some states prohibited price advertising, while others allowed virtually no information on eye examinations or eyeglasses to be disseminated for commercial purposes. These laws are alleged to be intended to protect consumers from fraudulent advertising affecting their health and to maintain professional standards among sellers and practitioners. Benham, who found eyeglass prices to be substantially lower in states that allowed advertising, estimates that the restrictions were reflected in prices ranging from 25 percent to more than 100 percent higher for what seemed to be products of the same quality. He concludes that it is established optometrists and other professionals within a state who benefit most from such restrictions.

125

Summation

Because it limited the economic powers of both the federal and the state governments and safeguarded the exercise of the commercial liberties, the U.S. Constitution preserved and guaranteed capitalism for this nation. The framers of the original document sought to create a society allowing free commerce in which the marketplace of goods and services was the ultimate economic authority. Their purpose of diffusing power and maximizing liberty could not have been achieved if this authority had rested with monarchs or majorities. The evidence indicates that the framers of the Fourteenth Amendment—Members of the Congress of 1866—were similarly motivated. The Supreme Court's contemporary policy according preference to the police power over the commercial liberties is not consistent with this design of government. Neither is the enormous growth of regulation, which has subordinated commercial pursuits to the legislative or administrative will.

Contemporary experience provides pragmatic support for the framers' belief in a capitalist economy. Individual liberties and the nation's economy seriously suffer from excessive economic regulation. A great deal of regulation has been sponsored by special interest groups to promote their own financial welfare, to the detriment of virtually all others. Studies indicate the results are not appreciably better from regulation adopted for more altruistic reasons. Whatever advantages the nation does obtain from regulation must be balanced against those disadvantages. The desirability of regulation must also be weighed against the substantial harm society sustains when government denies productive and creative people freedom to exercise their talents. Thus, a public policy that accepts economic regulation without maximum scrutiny can hardly be considered wise or beneficial.

To be sure, some economic restraints are essential to secure or achieve important societal interests. Restraints of this character have always been acceptable in this nation, whether they affect the economic, the intellectual, or the political arena. To permit the adoption of needed rules and exclude the rest requires that economic regulation be imposed only when strong and compelling justification for it exists. This standard is generally similar to that applied by the federal judiciary during the period of economic due process. It maintains on the whole the original intention in this area of the Constitution of 1787 and the Fourteenth Amendment. Contemporary experience evidences the soundness and desirability of this standard and therefore supports strict implementation of constitutional principles protecting the commercial liberties.

6

Capitalism or Democracy

Robert Lekachman

The Constitution and the Bill of Rights make two promises to Americans that have frequently clashed in the course of our national history. In recent years, their inherent incompatibility has become glaringly apparent. One commitment is to political equality, an implication that any individual's vote, effect upon his neighbors, and influence upon his elected representatives is approximately as important as another's. The second is an open invitation to all comers to enrich themselves by their own efforts. Political and economic markets overlap, however, and wealth translates into political influence, favorable legislation, and helpful decisions by bureaucrats. Rich people, not their poorer cousins, own newspapers, news magazines, and TV channels. The First Amendment protects a free press. To echo A. J. Liebling, only the wealthy own one. In the long run, political freedom cannot survive within the unfavoring context of plutocracy.

Why are we willing to endanger political freedom and equality for the sake of capitalism? Even capitalism's most sophisticated apologists readily concede that their preferred system lacks the glamour, awe, and mystery that customarily hedge the courts of kings and pontiffs. As Alfred Marshall remarked in speaking of human motivation, crass pursuit of profit by sellers and of individual gratification by their customers is notoriously consistent with the strongest but not the highest of personal impulses—with avarice, not altruism.[1]

[1] Sir Dennis Robertson quotes Marshall as follows: "Progress depends on the extent to which the *strongest* and not merely the *highest* forces of human nature can be utilised for the increase of social good." See Robert Lekachman, ed., *National Policy for Economic Welfare* (New York: Doubleday & Co., 1955), p. 2. A dissenter is George Gilder, who in *Wealth and Poverty* (New York: Basic Books, 1980) argues that capitalism is the most altruistic of modes of economic organization because investors necessarily risk resources without certainty of return.

In capitalism's favor, the theory of prices at its core offers a cheerful interpretation of the self-aggrandizing, maximizing choices of consumers and business enterprises. Conventional economic analysts customarily assert three celebratory claims. To begin with, free markets help to maximize not only profit but utility. Indeed, by the test of historical experience and the continuing example of alternative arrangements, a capitalist economy is the most efficient way to mobilize human and material resources and thus promote the steady growth of per capita output which translates into higher living standards for all. For St. Thomas Aquinas in the thirteenth century, the objective of economic activity was virtuous conduct conducive to salvation; times have changed, however. Steeped in the secularism of later eras, economists since Adam Smith have emphasized efficiency on earth as the central value of an economic system and the measure of its performance. When prices climb or decline in sensitive response to alterations in supply or demand, free of constraint from either private monopoly or government regulation, numerous economies occur. Managers substitute cheap machines for expensive labor, or cheap labor for expensive machines. Similar shuffles and reshuffles take place between amount of space and desirability of location, between plentiful and scarce materials, and so on, each shift reflecting determined pursuit of minimum cost and maximum profit. Excess profits, however, can endure only briefly, because the inexorable pressure of competition shoves prices and costs ever downward. Greedy businessmen scarcely nibble the carrot of profit before their jealous rivals snatch it away from them.

A second merit of capitalism is the personal liberty that accompanies unfettered choice. According to their fancy, individuals can spend or save, speculate or invest, emulate Mr. Micawber or Silas Marner. As entrepreneurs, men and women can chance their luck by starting new enterprises and, once in a long season, strike it rich after the fashion of Colonel Sanders with his Kentucky Fried Chicken, Ray Kroc with his billions of Big Macs, and the gene splicers of our own decade. If, as is considerably more likely, their enterprises fail or show only moderate success, the fault is their own.

The third and largest claim made for capitalism is political—the assertion that much more than coincidence is at work in the simultaneous expansion of capitalism and representative democracy in England and the United States since the Industrial Revolution. Although capitalism has also coexisted amiably with fascism and numerous contemporary authoritarian regimes, including those in Chile, Argentina, and the Union of South Africa, the claim does have some force. When the private sector is large and the public sphere commensurately small, few citizens need respect or fear the state as employer or landlord. When physicist Andrei Sakharov tested too severely the limited patience of Soviet rulers, they deprived him of his Moscow residence, university appointment, and access to friends and allies. In contrast, linguist Noam Chomsky, a valued member of the faculty of a distinguished private American university, continues to document the follies and crimes of his government without reprisal. Men and women accustomed to choosing their own merchandise, schools, personal and professional services, and living accommodations seem inclined to expect similar freedom to select legislators and presidents.

Proponents of market capitalism frequently ignore or minimize a severe weakness of this final claim—the fact that free markets disperse income and wealth in patterns not entirely consistent with political democracy. Professional sports stars, pop music idols, and the authors of best-selling novels amass fortunes because large numbers of their fellow citizens enthusiastically reward their performances. To its adherents, standard economics is a scoreboard on which people's unequal financial status appropriately reflects the wide range of their individual talents and energy. By implication, inequality of income and wealth is actually quite equitable. More than that: In the end, inequality promotes even the interests of the humble, unenterprising, and meagerly gifted because riches are the crucial lure that induces entrepreneurs to take risks, executives to scramble arduously up corporate ladders, and young people to undergo lengthy, frequently tedious professional training. Much as a rising tide lifts all boats, an expanding economy improves life for those at the bottom of the income distribution as well as for those at the top.

As the results of the 1980 presidential election suggest, many Americans endorse this perspective. As the misfortunes of George McGovern in 1972 and Fred Harris in 1976 appear to demonstrate, American politicians who brood publicly over the unequal distribution of wealth and advocate limiting inheritances fare badly as candidates for high office. Tax reformers too have come unhappily to realize that their repeated attempts to close tax loopholes that benefit the affluent usually wind up opening two new loopholes for each one they plug.

Here lurks an ambivalence in American attitudes. The Constitution, particularly as reinforced by the Fourteenth Amendment, proclaims strong guarantees of equality: trial by a jury of one's peers, freedom of speech and religion, and—magic phrase—equal protection. Section 1 of the Fourtenth Amendment prohibits any state from acting so as to "deny any person within its jurisdiction the equal protection of the laws."[2] Indeed, in 1866, two years before ratification of that amendment, an early civil rights act required that "all citizens of the United States shall have the same right . . . as is enjoyed by white citizens . . . to inherit, purchase, lease, sell, hold, and convey real and personal property."[3]

After a disgracefully long interval of political inertia or actual retrogression, Congress renewed the thrust toward racial equality in the Civil Rights Act of 1964. Title VII of the act extended assurances of equality beyond the black community by declaring it to be an "unlawful employment practice for an employer to fail or refuse to hire or to discharge any individual, or otherwise to discriminate against any individual, with respect to his compensation, terms, conditions, or privileges of employment because of such individual's race, color, religion, sex, or national origin."[4]

Foreign students of American life have almost universally noted —approvingly or otherwise—the equality of American manners and attitudes. Here is a typical passage from Alexis de Tocqueville:

> The more I advanced in the study of American society, the more I observed that . . . equality of condition is the fundamental fact from which all others seemed to be derived, and the central point at which all my observations terminated. . . . The gradual development of the principle of equality is, therefore, a providential fact. It has all the chief characteristics of such a fact: it is universal, it is lasting, it constantly eludes all human interference, and all events as well as all men contribute to its progress. . . . [It is] an irresistible revolution which has advanced for centuries in spite of every obstacle.[5]

The framers of our basic constitutional documents were serious people who must be credited with intending political entitlements to have consequences. Votes are shams unless they influence legislation. Free speech and press are meaningless if they do not shape public opinion. Fair trial by a jury of one's peers is mocked by the absence of adequate legal defense. This is to say that the Constitution started life as more

[2] See "The Constitution of the United States," reprinted in Paul Freund and others, Constitutional Law, 3d ed., 3 vols. (Boston: Little, Brown & Co., 1967), vol. 1, p. xviii.

[3] Ibid., vol. 2, p. 972.

[4] See M I. Sovern, Legal Restraints on Racial Discrimination in Employment (St. Paul, Minn.: West Publishing Co., 1973), p. 844.

[5] Democracy in America (New York: Alfred A. Knopf, 1945), vol. 1, p. 3.

than a capitalist document. The Founding Fathers were unwilling to attach the weight of dollars to political rights.

The pursuit of political equality, at least in the minimal form of fair chances to compete in a variety of markets, emerges as a passion of American radicals, liberals, conservatives, and, in extreme form, such libertarians as the philosopher Robert Nozick. Thus Chief Justice Warren Burger, the reactionary villain of Robert Woodward and Scott Armstrong's popular *The Brethren*, nevertheless proved himself alert to the racial effects of seemingly neutral tests and educational qualifications for employment and promotion by interpreting the 1964 statute as prohibiting "not only overt discrimination but also practices that are fair in form, but discriminatory in operation."[6]

The Supreme Court merits further discussion as the institution in our society most specifically charged with resolving the tension between a market economy that generates inequality and a body of fundamental law that insists on substantial equivalence among citizens of broadly differing financial status. At the most basic level, the Supreme Court has sniffed suspiciously at limitations on citizens' access to its own processes. In 1956, Justice Black affirmed the right of a duly convicted felon to a free transcript when this was required to appeal his conviction.[7] Seven years later, *Gideon* v. *Wainwright* extended *Griffin* by applying Sixth Amendment guarantees of counsel in serious criminal prosecutions to defendants in state courts.[8] The high court has been sufficiently committed to protecting the access of litigants to legal recourse, even in civil actions, to strike down a Connecticut requirement that divorce petitioners must pay court fees and costs for service of process. This requirement, the court contended, deprived married couples on welfare of the opportunity to dissolve unsatisfactory unions that was available to the financially better situated.

Well and good. But when money and property are at stake, the Court has historically leaned toward caution. Demands for equality couched in the language of equal protection make the Burger Court, like most of its predecessors, extremely uneasy. Thus, on the intricate issue of public-school financing, a majority rejected the conclusion of the California Supreme Court (and several other jurisdictions) that the equal protection language of both the federal and most state constitutions mandates equal public expenditure per pupil. In the landmark *San Antonio Independent School District* v. *Rodriguez*,

[6] See Griggs v. Duke Power Company, 401 U.S. 424 (1971), cited in Sovern, *Legal Restraints*, p. 886.

[7] Griffin v. Illinois, 351 U.S. 12 (1956).

[8] Gideon v. Wainwright, 373 U.S. 335 (1962).

Justice Powell argued that along with the usual criteria, such competing interests as traditions of local control had also to be weighed in the balance.[9] For education, the upshot was a minimum standard rather than an equal standard of protection, as states were empowered to spend substantially different amounts on variously located public-school children.

An even more illuminating example of the Supreme Court's reluctance to extend constitutional protection to the economic components of political and human rights concerns welfare payments. For a few years, during the brief sunshine of the Warren Court, the Supreme Court appeared determined to change the definition of welfare from gratuity to constitutionally protected right. Chief Justice Warren struck down substitute-father rules popular in Alabama and a number of other Southern states, asserting that Alabama's attempt to discourage illicit sexual activity and the birth of illegitimate infants "plainly conflicted with federal law and policy."[10] In other words, a woman could not be required to surrender the normal rights of Americans, including pursuit of sexual gratification and motherhood without benefit of holy matrimony, in order to qualify for public benefits.[11] In 1969 *Shapiro* v. *Thompson* conveyed a similar message to the North. Writing for the majority, Justice Brennan overturned a New York statute that imposed residency rules on welfare applicants, contending that unhampered travel is a basic right implied (though never stated) by the Constitution.[12]

Until the Supreme Court's astonishing majority holding in *Dandridge* v. *Williams* in 1970[13] advocates of welfare rights had been convinced that the justices were moving gradually but reliably toward definition of a new right—a guarantee of life on some minimum financial terms, protected by the complete constitutional panoply that shelters more traditional rights. In *Dandridge*, however, Justice Stewart, writing for a bare majority of the Court, upheld a Maryland maximum-grant statute that allowed states to treat large families less generously than small ones on pleas of fiscal exigency or other "rational" pretexts. (One school of judicial interpretation allows legislators generous leeway whenever they or sympathetic judges can discover some rational ground for their action.) Justices Marshall and

[9] San Antonio Independent School District v. Rodriguez, 411 U.S. 1 (1973).

[10] King v. Smith, 392 U.S. 309 (1968).

[11] Fussy concern for equity might suggest applying the same test, had it survived constitutional challenge, to the recipients of loan guarantees, crop subsidies, and similar tax-financed benefits.

[12] Shapiro v. Thompson, 394 U.S. 618 (1969).

[13] Dandridge v. Williams, 397 U.S. 471 (1970).

Brennan alone discerned a clear violation of equal protection in a rule that effectively curtailed living allowances for children (and adults) whenever a family numbered five or more children.

The following year, in *Wyman* v. *James,* Justice Blackmun, one of Richard Nixon's strict constructionists, abruptly reverted to the language of gratuity discarded by the Court in very recent precedents. The central issue of the case—whether a client could continue to receive welfare benefits after refusing home visits by a caseworker—involved Fourth Amendment prohibitions of unlawful searches and the "right of the people to be secure in their persons, houses, papers, and effects," which earlier Court decisions had held to be a basic right of a free society. In rejecting the applicability of the Fourth Amendment to Mrs. James's situation and thousands of similar ones, Justice Blackmun argued,

> One who dispenses purely private charity naturally has an interest in and expects to know how his charitable funds are utilized and put to work. The public, when it is the provider, rightly expects the same. It might well expect more, because of the trust aspect of public funds, and the recipient, as well as the caseworker, had not only an interest but an obligation.[14]

In the final days of its 1979–1980 term, the Supreme Court continued to retreat. In a 5 to 4 decision, it upheld the Hyde Amendment, which denied public Medicaid funds for most medically recommended abortions. Justice Stevens objected in dissent:

> If a woman has a constitutional right to place a higher value on avoiding either serious harm to her own health or perhaps an abnormal childbirth than on protecting potential life, the exercise of that right cannot provide the basis for the denial of a benefit to which she would otherwise be entitled. . . . One could with equal justification describe the right protected by the First Amendment as the right to make speeches without coercive interference by the Government and then sustain a Government subsidy for all medically needy persons except those who publicly advocate a change of administration.

Justice Marshall predicted with bitter directness that "the . . . result of the Hyde Amendment will be a significant increase in the number of poor women who will die or suffer significant health damage because of an inability to procure necessary medical services."[15]

14 Wyman v. James, 400 U.S. 309 (1971).
15 *New York Times,* July 1, 1980.

Constitutional Equity and Capitalist Disparity

I have lingered on such controversies as those over financing of public schools, rights to counsel, eligibility for welfare, and abortion because they exemplify the friction between the equality implied by constitutional guarantees and protections and the admitted, even flaunted, inequality of income and wealth generated by the normal operation of capitalist markets. To be rich is to increase the life chances of one's sons and daughters, to ensure the quality of one's legal representation in court proceedings,[16] to guarantee oneself the choice between abortion and carriage of a pregnancy to term, and to avoid ever facing Mrs. James's coerced choice between material benefit and exercise of constitutional right, among other advantages.

Pressure from private markets mocks constitutional guarantees of equality in other ways as well, and increases the unfortunate resemblance of political markets to commercial ones. Political scientists used to comfort themselves and their students more frequently than they probably do now with the heartening thought that the normal interplay of conflicting interest-group pressures prevents more than a temporary victory for any single group. Faintly incredible even when most in vogue, the veto groups of political pluralism have been laid to rest in an unmarked grave by none other than a reformed pluralist, Charles Lindblom, who in his magisterial *Politics and Markets* persuasively analyzed the dominion of business over American politics and culture.[17] As he accurately emphasized, business enjoys two shots at influencing political processes toward desired outcomes. In the first place, large corporations compete ideologically in the media (themselves large enterprises) both directly on their own behalf and in support of candidates whom they favor or who oppose officials they oppose. In addition, business occupies a uniquely favorable situation as the principal provider of jobs and incomes, which gives it a practical as well as an ideological lever.

In the ideological competition, the odds are heavy against critics of business, organized labor, consumer groups, and environmentalists

[16] Of Great Society programs, legal services for the poor has been among the most effective. Young, well-trained, and socially concerned attorneys have represented poor clients in a wide variety of civil and criminal cases. Their creative use of class actions has protected large groups against landlords, oppressive welfare administrators, and exploitative lenders and retailers. The Reagan administration's proposal to eliminate legal services in civil cases will, if endorsed by Congress, widen even more the resource gap between landlords and tenants, lenders and borrowers, and sellers and buyers.

[17] *Politics and Markets* (New York: Basic Books, 1977).

for reasons both self-evident and slightly less apparent. Money purchases Mobil and Exxon "informational" advertisements on editorial pages all over the country, including the eminent Op-Ed page of the *New York Times*. Corporate cash sponsors Milton Friedman's television series "Free to Choose" and promotes the book based upon it, as well as Ben Wattenberg's series in celebration of the status quo. Fewer and fewer newspapers are independently owned; more and more are units in chains that dispense meticulously balanced samples of columnists about as far left as (but no farther than) Mary McGrory and about as far right as (but no farther than) George Will. When has a genuine radical—perhaps Paul Sweezy, the dean of Marxist economists—last been interviewed on public or commercial television? It is an old story that the mass media operate so as to narrow the boundaries of political choice. So long as Dan Rather, John Chancellor, and the network staffs behind them determine what is news and who are acceptable exponents of opinion, neither the American Left nor the individualist Right is likely to emerge into the general public perception.

This is not to fall into the pat generalization that the media are universally bankrupt. It is comforting and important that *The Nation, Monthly Review, The Progressive, Dissent, Inquiry,* and other small-circulation journals continue to appear at regular intervals. Now and again they have influenced politicians and public policies. Fairly often, the mass media pick up stories from the minority press which they then purvey in attenuated form to large audiences. All this said, it is still sad truth that the day-to-day flow of information and opinion echoes business values in loud tones and others sotto voce if at all. Even the *New York Times* is a commercial enterprise in the last resort, dependent for survival on advertising.

Inequality promotes conservative causes. If tax initiatives designed for reform routinely yield benefits to affluent stockholders and corporations, if even in time of fiscal austerity subsidies to shipbuilders, owners of corporate jets, commercial farmers, and badly managed auto and steel companies continue to draw congressional approval, if public rage against Exxon and its peers translates mysteriously not into nationalization, divestiture, or stringent public regulation but into an exceedingly mild windfall profits tax, and if the principal results of tax revolts along the lines of California's Proposition 13 are benefits for businessmen, the causes are not far to seek, and astonishment is for the naive.

Particularly when unemployment is high and rising, business wields to maximum advantage its second edge over competing interests. Corporations auction themselves off to communities in need of jobs and taxes by offering to locate new plants or corporate head-quarters in that fortunate municipality which designs the most lucrative package of subsidies, tax remissions, and relaxation of onerous regulations.[18] Open-shop states all but trumpet the docility of grateful workers heartwarmingly eager to perform hard labor for low rewards. Chairmen of boards also threaten to desert struggling older communities in the Northeast and industrial Middle West unless their mayors and city councils match competing propositions. One of the infrequently mentioned sources of New York City's minor revival is its progressive change into a low-wage community graced with sweatshops in Chinatown and portions of outlying boroughs.

It is no exaggeration, then, to conclude that the potent combination of business domination of the media and corporate manipulation of public fears of losing jobs and income substantially constricts political freedom. Much of the stuff of politics concerns the design of tax, spending, and regulatory policies, over which business exerts tacit vetoes. Once more New York City is a strong case in point. As the price of rescue from imminent bankruptcy in the spring of 1975, the metropolis's elected officials were compelled to share their authority over taxing and spending with a Financial Control Board and Municipal Assistance Corporation administered by and for the commercial and business community. The not unexpected result is that public transportation is a shamble, uncollected garbage piles up, local streets are pitted with potholes, and fire companies' response time to alarms has lengthened ominously.

In an already conservative polity, the victory in 1980 of a candidate more conservative than Barry Goldwater is a testimonial to public willingness to meet the terms of organized business out of hope that benefits will sift down to average families.

The Economic Struggle

Much as jurists have avoided promulgating constitutional principles of equity in economic cases, free-market economists have seldom extended to political markets their lovingly crafted analysis of con-

---

[18] Detroit, most desperately afflicted by the troubles of the auto industry, has exercised its power of eminent domain to destroy an integrated neighborhood nicknamed Poletown to provide a site for a new Cadillac factory. As the chairman of General Motors explained on national television, Detroit was not subsidizing his company but merely providing the equivalent of the green field in which a new plant could have been built in the absence of Detroit's action.

sumer and corporate maximization. Economists are conservative souls trained in a severe intellectual discipline which ignores history and passes lightly over much of contemporary sociological reality. As most ordinary folk without the benefit of graduate training in economics probably realize, however, consumers do not maximize in the abstract. They make decisions within a context created by sellers, among whom competition is drastically limited by a clutch of monopolies, oligopolies, and tacit price-rigging arrangements. During the Carter years, for example, the steel industry sought and won trigger-price protection from its more efficient foreign rivals. Since Reagan's election, the automobile industry has extracted "voluntary" agreements from Japanese producers to limit their alarmingly successful invasion of the American market. For large corporations, it frequently makes better sense to lobby in Washington and state capitols than to improve the efficiency of their operations or the quality of their products.

Back when the going was good and the American economy grew at an annual rate of 3 percent per capita, it was possible for both the laity and professional economists to neglect, if not ignore, immanent discrepancies between political and commercial market assumptions and behavior. For a number of substantial reasons, however, the going has ceased to be good, and matters are unlikely soon to improve. Naturally the energy coup pulled off by the Organization of Petroleum Exporting Countries (OPEC) heads any list of developments depressing to economic growth.[19] Whatever progress domestic suppliers make with coal, nuclear energy, synthetic fuels, or solar power, energy is certain to be expensive for at least the remainder of this century. Accordingly, American resources will continue to be transferred to various combinations of foreign and domestic energy suppliers—a substantial charge on the increments this country can hope to attain in its gross national product.[20]

[19] The $90-100 billion OPEC bill can be regarded as a subtraction from growth attainable by the United States, much like a tax imposed and collected by foreigners rather than the domestic government.

[20] From the standpoint of the energy-importing Northeast and Midwest, little distinguishes domestic oil- and gas-exporting regions within the United States from OPEC. In both instances rising world market prices extract additional resources from purchasers and accelerate the drift of industry and population to the Sunbelt. *Urban America in the Eighties,* one of the reports of President Carter's Commission for a National Agenda for the Eighties (the McGill Commission), regards this drift as both inevitable and potentially advantageous to national growth. Insofar as it is stimulated by the impact of cartel policies, these regional gains and losses are distinctly artificial, not in the least "inevitable."

Against the national income account there are at least three additional debits. The terms of competition between the United States and the Soviet Union for global hegemony, and the internal rivalries among the members of the European Economic Community, Japan, and our own country, render it all but unavoidable that some portion of the third world's bill to the industrialized first world will be reluctantly paid. In crude terms, the Soviet Union competes with the West by offering arms to the developing world and the advisers to use them. The West, including Japan, offers benefits of much greater value, among them the items on the complete third world economic agenda. These include preferential access to the markets of the rich Northern Hemisphere, transfers of capital and technology on concessional terms, financing of petroleum imports, stabilization of commodity prices, and equitable exploitation of the resources beneath the ocean floor—items destined very soon to levy substantial costs on the United States. Thus rivalry will raise the price of raw materials and manufactured goods from developing countries; it may well increase taxes to finance foreign assistance, though probably in disguised forms,[21] and it probably will further limit the improvements Americans can hope to achieve in their own living standards. The justice of these claims, moreover, has little bearing on the likelihood that some of them will be acceded to.[22]

A third debit against American growth falls under the rubric of externalities, the unemotive term of art which embraces emotional events like the contamination of Love Canal and the Three Mile Island accident. Externalities are costs imposed on individuals or communities without their consent (or, more rarely, benefits conferred in the absence of any request for them) by profit-making enterprises. They typically occur when companies are able to shuffle off some of their business costs on communities, as when a town is compelled to raise tax money to cleanse streams and atmosphere polluted by a

---

[21] When Chase Manhattan, Citibank, and their domestic and European peers reschedule loans to developing countries as the alternative to outright default, they lengthen repayment schedules, reduce interest rates, and, on occasion, forgive portions of the principal. Particularly if their loans are backed by government guarantees, these arrangements are tantamount to resource shifts from lenders to foreigners—semantic substitutes for old-fashioned foreign aid.

[22] The issue is a great deal more complex than unsophisticated opponents of imperialism and advocates of first world reparations to their former colonies in the third world usually admit. When foreign aid is financed directly or indirectly from tax levies on middle- and working-class citizens in the first world and transferred to small third world elites, whether of the authoritarian Left or the equally authoritarian Right, the transfers are from relatively poor to relatively rich *individuals*, not from rich to poor countries.

steel mill, utility, or similar enterprises, or on individuals, as when people are burdened with medical bills for damage inflicted by pollution, adulterated products, or unwholesome working conditions.

In response to public clamor, Congress from the mid-1960s onward has reluctantly compelled business enterprises, large and small, to invest substantial sums in safety equipment, water cleansing devices, smokestack scrubbers, and quality control. Currently under heavy attack as unduly cumbersome and burdensome to American enterprise, the regulatory legislation represents billions of dollars substracted from the capital available to develop new products and, consequently, from the growth rate of the gross national product (GNP).[23] The GNP is not, of course, a sacred—or even highly reliable—index of the quality of life. An increase in cigarette sales enlarges measured GNP, and so does the cost of treating the additional victims of smoking-related ailments. National income accountants neglect to estimate the value of improved air and water quality, or the extra life earnings realizable from reductions in highway casualty rates attributable to government-imposed safety requirements. Still, both externalities and their current remedies are indisputable drags on the money available to individuals, communities, and businesses for more productive uses.

Women, blacks, Hispanics, and Native Americans have presented American society with yet another set of overdue bills, the final subtraction from measurable growth. This is affirmative action. In the long run, affirmative action policies pursued with conviction and intelligence certainly could be expected to stimulate economic growth, simply by enlarging the pool of human talent from which employers routinely draw. For the short run, however, the prospects are not promising. Given eroding public support and (to echo Thorstein Veblen) conscientious business sabotage, it is likely, though difficult to establish quantitatively, that the net effect of current policies to rectify discrimination in hiring and promoton is negative.

In addition to its direct economic impact, slow growth increases the friction between the promise of political and constitutional equality and the gross fact of economic inequality. In the past, during periods of rapid economic growth, people who perceived that friction were usually unperturbed, because they expected themselves—or, at worst,

---

[23] Washington University's Murray Weidenbaum, a specialist in the economics of regulation before he became chairman of the Council of Economic Advisers early in 1981, calculated the annual cost of regulation to the private sector at a cool $100 billion. Athough that number has been frequenty disputed, it has also been approvingly cited many times, not least prestigiously by President Reagan.

their children—ultimately to benefit from financial inequality and to wield more than their share of political influence. When in 1906 Werner Sombart asked a question which has not ceased to haunt the radical Left—"Why is there no socialism in the United States?"—the burden of his answer stressed the reality of social, economic, and occupational mobility and, most potent of all, the evocative power of the myth of unlimited opportunity.[24]

That myth is less credible in the 1980s than at any time since the Great Depression of the 1930s. As working-class and lower middle-class families have begun painfully to comprehend, college degrees have been devalued, and elite professional training is far too expensive for all but a few of their most gifted sons and daughters. The cessation or slowing of growth reinforces the reality of corporate power indirectly as well as overtly. When jobs are scarce, confused and frightened employees grow more and more attached to their presumptive benefactors, their employers. As rival providers, unions steadily lose legitimacy. Samuel Gompers's celebrated concise definition of labor's aims—"More"—handicaps unions whenever, as in recent years, "more" cannot be delivered by even the most bellicose of union negotiators save at the price of lost jobs, plant closings, and a shift of other plants to nonunion locations.

The Political Struggle

Political parties on the right are peopled mainly by the affluent and those who hope to join them. Socialist and social-democratic parties, on the other hand, traditionally have drawn their recruits from men and women who attach their own aspirations to the improved fortunes of the group of which they are a part. Thus, as awareness spreads that the prospects for individual riches have drastically diminished, the times are likely to become receptive at last to the emergence of a credible Left.[25] Because without hope, life is intolerable, I choose to assume that after the conservative interlude represented by the Reagan administration, American politics will gradually polarize around credible conservative and radical alternatives.

---

[24] Werner Sombart, *Why Is There No Socialism in the United States?* tr. Patricia M. Hocking and C. T. Husbands (White Plains, N.Y.: M. E. Sharpe, 1976).

[25] An obvious alternative is to drift into some variety of corporate authoritarianism, the apprehension of Robert L. Heilbroner and Bertram Gross. See Heilbroner's *Inquiry into the Human Prospect*, expanded ed. (New York: W. W. Norton & Co., 1974), and Gross's *Friendly Fascism* (New York: M. Evans & Co., 1980).

To be an optimist in 1981 or 1982, an American must cultivate the capacity to look beyond 1984 and see visions of a society quite different from Orwell's nightmare.

At the beginning of such speculations, it is well to be brief and tentative. To start with, it is worth mentioning that conventional economics has been discredited by the test of its own market. A thinner-skinned set of professional practitioners would have been shamed into silence long since by errors of diagnosis and prophecy so numerous and glaring. Notoriously, standard economics, whether Keynesian or monetarist, has groped uncertainly with inflation, unemployment, and international economic relations. Its newest off-spring, the supply-side theology, scarcely warrants discussion; it is a wager placed with religious fervor on the capacity of human avarice to revitalize declining industries, renew historical rates of growth, and, ultimately, improve general living standards. Like any other strongly held faith, supply-side economics persist in spite of both the absence of evidence for it and the presence of evidence against it.

Among a growing number of economists, many of them young, a revival of Marxist and institutionalist approaches holds some promise of intellectual progress. So does the Cambridge (England) paradigm associated with Joan Robinson and her followers among radical Keynesians.

While they are waiting for the economists to regroup, radicals can advance along two paths toward the goal of reconstructing markets for lawyers and politicians. The first and less promising path continues efforts by partisans of Ralph Nader and Common Cause to conform the legal and political markets more closely to the egalitarian promises of constitutional law. For politicians, this might mean three-week presidential campaigns, exclusion of television as an electioneering tool (or controlled access to it on fair terms), and restrictions on political campaign spending as severe as those of Great Britain. For lawyers, the possibilities include combining free counsel for the legally indigent and cheap help for those somewhat better off with the requirement that every attorney, as a condition of membership in the bar, accept cases by lottery or according to a judicially supervised roster. If some accused mugger were blessed with the services of Edward Bennett Williams or F. Lee Bailey and an indicted antitrust violator lumbered with the "help" of a low-ranking recent graduate from a third-rate law factory, so much the better for human dignity. If not true equality before the law, such an arrangement at least would provide a distribution of benefits by a more democratic principle than relative wealth.

The second and substantially superior path toward harmonizing two major markets so differently constructed is, of course, to transform the character of private ownership. As a legal realist, I do not think that constitutional amendment is a prerequisite to such a transformation. A sympathetic president, our own François Mitterrand, will appoint the appropriate jurists. As has been their historical custom, the justices of the Supreme Court will heed the lessons of the last election. I can do no more than briefly sketch the possibilities and a few of the dilemmas. As the contrasting recent histories of Sweden and England illustrate, nationalization alone—particularly when it is limited to a country's financial lemons (aptly dubbed citrus socialism)—does nothing to diminish inequality, stimulate democracy in the workplace, or enhance the prospects for local self-determination. For more than a generation, Sweden has been both more efficient and less inegalitarian than England, even though the public sector is substantially larger in the latter than the former.

Among radicals, there is a generational argument between middle-aged proponents of national planning and younger enthusiasts for decentralization experiments under the control of workers or the community. From my vantage point as one of the first group, the younger radicals who enliven such journals as *Mother Jones* and *Working Papers* seem thus far to have failed to grapple with major problems of coordination and equitable distribution. A volume such as Kirkpatrick Sale's *Human Scale* amounts to a useful encyclopedia of instances in which small is not merely beautiful but technically and economically viable into the bargain.[26] Neither Sale nor his sympathizers demonstrate, however—nor, to be fair, do they claim—that 225 million Americans could subsist at an acceptable standard of comfort on their own labors in a large number of decentralized, "human-scale" communities. If somehow they could, moreover, would radicals of any age and disposition tolerate the spectacle of successful communities bordered by nearly destitute ones? That some would fail is almost inevitable—and so is the responding cry for subsidization of the poor by the affluent. In short order, government would resume its traditional functions of collecting and redistributing revenue, and shortly afterward setting standards for the disbursement of reshuffled tax proceeds. It is the weakness of good-hearted writers such as Sale, in the utopian tradition of Robert Owen and the twentieth-century guild socialists, that they simply ignore the crucial issues posed by their preference for small-scale productive activity

[26] Kirkpatrick Sale, *Human Scale* (New York: Coward, McCann & Geoghegan, 1980).

organized around small communities. How in interdependent societies that operate through increasingly intricate divisions of labor
can small communities operate at all? And if somehow they do,
how can they arrange to perform the essential integrative communal,
redistributive, and allocative functions of central government?

I am able to stack the deck in my own favor this way because
the devotees of national planning in the American context have
done little more than brood from time to time on adaptations of
French and especially Japanese mechanisms. In those native habitats,
indicative planning is distinctly conservative. Government-business
alliances run the show. Unions and other organized interests are
assigned minor roles. This, indeed, is the sort of planning intelligent
corporate types such as Felix Rohatyn envisage.[27] Rohatyn's central
idea is a revived Reconstruction Finance Corporation, equipped with
a mandate to design coherent policies in favor of growing, efficient
industries.

Business Week took a similar tack when it devoted its June 30,
1980, issue to the topic "Reindustrialization of America." The
editors' focus was on a social contract supposedly signed by representatives of business, government, labor, environmentalists, consumer advocates, and minorities. They must have hoped that politicians, labor leaders, and corporate executives would be attracted by
the idea of a social contract. At this writing no recruits have signed
up. As candid as it is intelligent, the magazine presented its position
bluntly: "The drawing of a social contract must take precedence over
the aspirations of the poor, the minorities, and the environmentalists."
Government was to smooth the route to revitalization by relaxing
regulations, altering antitrust laws that "interfere with the ability of
U.S. companies to compete effectively with other countries—especially Germany and Japan—in world markets," [28] revising the Internal
Revenue Code on behalf of business, and creating a wholesome

[27] Watchers of the New York literary scene in 1980 and 1981 were intrigued by
the frequent appearance of Rohatyn in the pages of the *New York Review of
Books*, an excellent indicator of cultural fashions in the metropolis. Situated
vaguely on the literary and political left, the *New York Review* has been traditionally hospitable to many shades of radical opinion. Its encouragement of
an unashamed capitalist gives one cause to ponder the ideological stability of
the journal's editors, its contributors, or both.

[28] MIT economist Lester Thurow, usually identified with the Democratic Left
and Michael Harrington's Democratic Socialist Organizing Committee, also
advocates substantial revision of antitrust barriers to the formation of units
large enough to compete in world markets with Japanese trading companies
and Western European cartels—another example of the occasional convergence
of the planning wing of the corporate community with the Left.

environment for corporate activity in other ways. *Business Week* expressed confidence that as these measures began to take hold, their beneficial consequences would filter down to ordinary wage slaves in the shape of more real income out of a faster-growing, more fully employed, and less inflationary economy.

This is not, I hardly need say, a version of indicative planning I can enthusiastically contemplate. But in principle there is no reason why, in the administration of a far more successful George McGovern, Fred Harris, or Ted Kennedy, the tax, credit, spending, and planning levers could not be wielded in the service of other than corporate priorities. I envisage a mode of planning that converts the full-employment rhetoric of the Humphrey-Hawkins Act into the creation of jobs in the public sector.[29] I can imagine a redesign of the Internal Revenue Code aimed at the dispersal of large fortunes, the single most promising way to diminish inequality. A wealth-acquisition tax would be an admirable substitute for the existing baffling complexities of inheritance-tax law. However well equipped with affluent parents or other relatives, any heir could be limited over his or her lifetime to the inheritance of a stated sum, perhaps $200,000 (I am prepared to negotiate the figure).

The crucial question of efficient scale I leave open for future inquiry. Insofar as it appears feasible to generate solar energy economically with solar panels and photovoltaic cells, I support recasting federal credit, contract, research, and development priorities to encourage those forms in preference to large-scale solar devices such as satellites and towers. Agriculture also appears to be an industry in which the advantages of scale decline very rapidly. On the other hand, if in our improved, less unequal future society, we still yearn to fly long distances, we must in all probability reconcile ourselves to continuing to assemble enormous 747s in gigantic factories.

Radicals of the Left need to appraise the menu of democratic approaches that might be used in factories and offices. The United Automobile Workers' Douglas Fraser can be wished the best of good fortune on the Chrysler board of directors, and the workers who have secured control of bankrupt Rath meatpacking plants can be wished the same, while dangerous parallels with English experience in the socialization of failing enterprises and industries are being noted. When their financial and market situation is sufficiently desperate,

---

[29] Passed late in 1978, the act has been an exceedingly well-kept secret. Its unemployment targets—4 percent general unemployment and 3 percent adult unemployment by 1985—were mentioned by none of the candidates in the 1980 presidential contest.

corporate managers become advocates of "citrus socialism" avid for help from union devils, bungling government bureaucrats, Saudi princes, or anyone else with an available bundle of cash. When experiments in workers' control occur under such desperately adverse circumstances, chances are that the outcome will be slightly delayed insolvency, and an approach will be discredited which in more propitious circumstances might well have succeeded.

The Path Ahead

In the remainder of this century, Americans are likely to face a stark choice between extending current trends toward unchecked plutocracy and encouraging the emergence of an effective democratic political Left. Plutocracy, it has been the burden of my argument, is certain to swamp the legal and constitutional structures that incorporate traditional guarantees of individual liberty and independent action into our polity. The triumph of overt conservative ideology in the 1980 presidential and congressional races may be cause for optimism, then, in that it has had the effect of legitimizing coherent politics of a different variety. The kind of politics that animated the 1980 elections was staunchly ideological. All politics implies the ordering and representation of inconsistent interests. Ideological politics has the useful quality of making explicit the reasons why some objectives and interests are to be preferred to others.

In Richard Tawney's famous definition, socialism is about equality. Hence the democratic socialist alternative ought to start with a redistribution of income and wealth. I believe that existing disparities, particularly of wealth, threaten the health of representative institutions and individual liberties and serve no useful function. Or, to put it another way, Americans probably would contribute the same productive energies to an economy with a much narrower spread between the incomes of blue-collar workers and chief executive officers. Great wealth is not an irreplaceable motivator. It does, however, exert great and pervasive influence. Manhattan, for example, is an island shaped by the preferences of a single family, the Rockefellers. Their monuments include the World Trade Center, Rockefeller Center, the United Nations, Riverside Church, the Cloisters, the Museum of Modern Art, and the entire Wall Street area. Great museums and architectural gems ornament this list, as well as some substantial architectural mistakes. The point at issue, however, is the legitimacy of shaping a city's profile not according to democratic choice but rather as a reflection of the power of wealth.

145

How much equality do we need? More. The answer is empirical: One pushes in the direction of equal rewards and assets until incentives to work, invest, and start new ventures begin visibly to diminish. John Stuart Mill, in the middle of the last century, opposed progressive income taxes because he feared they would weaken people's incentive to work. For the same reason, he supported heavy levies on inheritances as stimuli to the work efforts of heirs. As I have suggested, a wealth-acquisition tax might be an excellent place to begin.

Socialists need to develop sophisticated notions of appropriate planning. Where technology dictates large-scale organization, an appropriate response is federal incorporation of the enterprise. This is the minimal approach we should take to bringing Exxon and its peers under social control. The energy giants should be prohibited from acquiring dominion over coal, solar experimentation, and nuclear sources and be required to divest themselves of their acquisitions to date. A government agency should act as the nation's buying agent in all dealing with OPEC.

Where an industry is failing, as is the case with housing and the health sector, a different kind of intervention is called for. Most Americans are priced out of the new-home and rental markets. The pace of inflation in the health industry is twice that of the consumer price index. Even according to conservative canons, the case is clear for reorganization of these major components of the economy. In housing and health, as in energy, the current entrepreneurial forms could effectively be replaced with mixtures of cooperative, union-sponsored or community-sponsored, and public-operated services. Such arrangements imply—as they should—effective social control over investments as well, including shifts of enterprises within the country and out of the country.

The most egalitarian of economic policies, and the most friendly to renewed growth where it is possible, is a full-employment policy which deploys the tools of active intervention in the labor market, including guarantees of publicly created jobs. To redeem the forgotten promises of the 1978 Humphrey-Hawkins Full Employment and Balanced Growth Act will require a coherent and permanent incomes policy. It should be government's task to supervise key prices and wage bargains, with the aid of any of several approaches: mandatory standards; an equitable social compact among labor, management, and the public; tax-based incomes policies.

Although my aspirations may smack of the fruitlessly utopian at present, I have enough confidence in both the strength of democratic tradition and the weakness of the plutocratic approach to solving our economic afflictions to expect that as current exercises in nostalgia prove increasingly disappointing, and as the inequity of current policies impresses itself even on some of their beneficiaries, American politics will awaken from its long slumber and the Left will rise again. Unless it does, the contest between market inequity and political equality will terminate disastrously.

7

The Constitution and the Spirit of Commerce

Stephen Miller

In recent years it has become commonplace for observers of American politics to argue that the American form of representative government works poorly and needs to be changed. Some intellectuals, mainly those on the Left, favor radical change. Elsewhere in this volume Walter Dean Burnham speaks of the "radical defectiveness of the existing constitutional order as a framework for creating and sustaining comprehensive social and economic policy." And Sheldon Wolin has said recently that the country needs a "long revolution, aimed at deconstituting the present structure of power"—a revolution that will lead to "new forms, new scales, new beings."[1]

Most Americans, however, are less disposed to welcoming radical change than to finding ways of making representative government more efficient. Many Americans, I suspect, probably agree that "the representative systems of North America, Europe and elsewhere . . . are too slow, too inefficient, too undemocratic for our times."[2] Both left-wing and right-wing populists think such measures as referendums and initiatives will not only speed up the decision-making process, they will also make the process more democratic. Such measures, it is also assumed, will thwart the power of special interests to shape legislation. Others are suspicious of such populist forms of decision making, but want to find ways of weakening Congress in order to strengthen the power of the executive branch.

One can understand why many Americans think that the so-called deadlock of democracy requires that, at the very least, we reexamine the constitutional system to see whether it is still capable

[1] "The People's Two Bodies," *democracy*, vol. 1, no. 1 (January 1981), p. 24.
[2] F. M. Esfandiary, "Old Planet, New World," *New York Times*, October 12, 1979, p. A31.

of ensuring the safety and prosperity of the nation. In the 1780s, when the system was put into effect, the United States was a relatively small, coastal, predominantly agrarian country of approximately 4 million people; two hundred years later it is a large, continental, highly industrialized global superpower of more than 225 million. Many Americans—if they think about the framers at all—assume that their vision is at least partially out of date. Yet far from being irrelevant, the vision of the framers, as it is elucidated in *The Federalist*—a collection of essays that James Madison called "the most authentic exposition of the text of the federal constitution"—can help to clarify the way contemporary questions of political economy are discussed. Looking back at *The Federalist* may make it possible to move beyond certain stock assumptions of contemporary political discourse inherited from the nineteenth century—assumptions that are no longer illuminating or useful.

Aims and Expectations of the Framers

The first question that needs to be asked is: What did the framers intend? Perhaps the sharpest recent attack on the representative system devised by the framers has been by Lawrence Goodwyn, a well-known historian of American populism. According to Goodwyn, the Constitution was a scheme advanced by an elite group of merchants and bankers "to fashion . . . undemocratic structures of monetary and taxation policy." Goodwyn compares the framers' scheme to the scheme of Lenin in 1917: just as the Bolsheviks overthrew the democratic regime of Kerensky, so the framers overthrew the democratic regime of the Confederation. As Goodwyn says, "Anticipating Lenin by 120 years, they decided, in the name of their own understanding of political values, that the democratic polity could not be trusted." This conservative solution, Goodwyn argues, of "rule by a more or less enlightened commercial elite is undemocratic in its very premises, as is the Leninist formulation of an ideological elite."[3]

Goodwyn's understanding of the framers' intentions closely resembles that of Charles Beard, who argued seventy years ago, in *An Economic Interpretation of the Constitution*, that the framers devised the Constitution in order to protect their own economic interests. Virtually all American historians have rejected Beard's analysis, calling it crude and simple-minded. But Goodwyn's analysis

[3] "Organizing Democracy: The Limits of Theory and Practice," *democracy*, vol. 1, no. 1 (January 1981), pp. 57-59.

goes even further than Beard's, for Beard never went so far as to compare the framers to Lenin; Lenin, after all, ruthlessly crushed all those who disagreed with him. Yet even if Goodwyn's analysis of the framers' intentions is rejected, there is a sense in which Goodwyn is right: The framers were not proponents of pure or direct democracy. They were in favor of a representative government in which "the cool and deliberate sense of the community" would "ultimately prevail," but in which "the people in their collective capacity" are "totally" excluded from "any share" in the government.[4]

The authors of The Federalist, Madison, Alexander Hamilton, and John Jay, were quite clear about why they opposed democracy— opposed, that is, a government run directly by the people rather than by men chosen by the people to be their representatives. Democracies, Madison said, "have ever been spectacles of turbulence and contention; have ever been found incompatible with personal security or the rights of property; and have in general been as short in their lives as they have been violent in their deaths."[5] Democracies bred the related diseases of majority faction and violent faction, both of which could bring about the destruction of liberty. The state governments of the Confederation were not democracies, but they were more democratic than the framers liked and their democratic turbulence disturbed the framers, who thought the new American republic might fall apart—anarchy leading eventually to tyranny. "The more I see, the more I find reason for those who love this country to weep over its blindness," Hamilton wrote in 1782.[6] And Madison argued in 1785 that unless the union were strengthened, the disunited states would become "the sport of foreign politics, threaten the very existence of liberty, and blast the glory of the Revolution." The weaknesses of the new republic, he feared, would cause it to "tumble to the ground."[7]

Not all Americans were so worried about the future of the republic, but many Americans did think that the republic was in danger; George Washington was probably expressing a common opinion when he wrote to John Jay in 1786 to complain about the "astonishing changes" of the past few years. "I am told," he said,

[4] The Federalist, no. 63, ed. Clinton Rossiter (New York: New American Library, 1961), p. 387.

[5] The Federalist, no. 10, p. 81.

[6] Quoted in Richard B. Morris, ed., The Basic Ideas of Alexander Hamilton (New York: Pocket Library, 1957), p. 76.

[7] Quoted in Douglass Adair, Fame and the Founding Fathers, ed. Trevor Colbourn (New York: W. W. Norton & Co., 1974), p. 134.

"that even respectable characters speak of a monarchical form of government without horror. . . . What a triumph for the advocates of despotism to find that we are incapable of governing ourselves. . . . Would to God that wise measures may be taken in time to avert the consequences we have but too much reason to apprehend."[8] Many Europeans, even those well-disposed to the new American republic, agreed with these gloomy assessments. Joseph Priestley, an English radical Whig and American sympathizer, said that "it was taken for granted that the moment Americans had thrown off the yoke of Great Britain, the different states would go to war among themselves."[9]

Worried about the future of the republic, the framers of the Constitution read deeply in history and political philosophy in the hope of finding some way to ensure the health of the regime. Their reading of history gave them little cause for optimism, for republican governments rarely had been stable. Hamilton alluded to the violent history of ancient republics, alternating "between extremes of tyranny and anarchy," and admitted that "if it had been found impracticable to have devised models of a more perfect structure, the enlightened friends of liberty would have been obliged to abandon the cause of that species of government [that is, republican] as indefensible."[10] It was not their reading in history but their reading in political philosophy—especially eighteenth-century political philosophy—that gave them cause for hope.

According to Hamilton, "the science of politics . . . has received great improvement," and as a result of that improvement "the excellence of republican government may be retained and its imperfections lessened or avoided."[11] The science of politics offered a remedy that would reduce the possibility of majority faction and violent faction without subverting liberty. The remedy, of course, was a political one—the creation of a strong national government—but it was also an economic one; the republic would become strong and stable only if it were a predominantly commercial polity. For the central conclusion of those who advocated a science of politics was that only in predominantly commercial polities could liberty flourish without leading to violent civil discord.

---

[8] Washington to Jay, in Richard Hofstadter, ed., *Great Issues in American History* (New York: Random House, 1958), p. 83.

[9] Priestley quoted in Adair, *Fame and the Founding Fathers*, p. 117.

[10] *The Federalist*, no. 9, pp. 71-72.

[11] Ibid.

The Science of Politics

In the eighteenth century, "science" referred not to what we now call the sciences, but to any uniform body of knowledge. The eighteenth-century "scientists of politics" took their model from biology rather than mathematics. They were less interested in deducing the nature of justice than in classifying the numerous regimes that had existed in the world in the hope of arriving at some general laws about politics. And they were especially interested in coming up with remedies for a political problem that had preoccupied Thomas Hobbes—the problem of faction. The eighteenth-century scientists of politics, it could be said, all worked under the shadow of Hobbes. They were persuaded by him of the centrality of the problem of faction, but they wanted a solution that was different from Hobbes's.

Hobbes had come to the conclusion that factions could not be allowed to flourish in a polity because they would inevitably lead to violent civil discord. Man, Hobbes said, was prone to be violent about matters of opinion. Only an absolute monarch, he argued, can resolve such differences of opinion peacefully; only an absolute monarch can guarantee security and tranquillity. Although virtually all Englishmen rejected Hobbes's solution to the problem of faction, since it meant the destruction of liberty, many Englishmen thought factions were bad for the health of the polity. Factions, it was argued, might not cause violent civil discord, but they made it difficult for citizens to think about the common good of the country.

During the first half of the eighteenth century, the most influential opponent of faction was Viscount Bolingbroke, a prolific pamphleteer who was a close friend of such writers as Jonathan Swift and Alexander Pope. Bolingbroke's argument was very different from Hobbes's. Whereas Hobbes thought that factions are inevitable, Bolingbroke saw them as the result of "the spirit of private interest."[12] If men would only take a disinterested view of the public interest, he argued, then factions would disappear. Because Bolingbroke was regarded as a defender of the landed aristocracy, and thus a member of a faction himself, his arguments were dismissed by many Englishmen as the purest humbug. Bolingbroke, however, did not think his position inconsistent or hypocritical, for he thought that only the landed aristocracy were capable of a disinterested view of the common good because only they were free

---

[12] Quoted in Isaac Kramnick, *Bolingbroke and His Circle: The Politics of Nostalgia in the Age of Walpole* (Cambridge: Harvard University Press, 1968), p. 79.

from commercial attachments. The key point is that Bolingbroke viewed with alarm the growth of commerce in general and, more specifically, the increasing power of commercial men.

In this dispute, a third view began to develop. Those who advocated a science of politics disagreed both with Hobbes's belief in the inevitability of violent factional discord if liberty were allowed to flourish and with Bolingbroke's fears that commerce was undermining the health of Britain. Commerce, they argued, made liberty and tranquillity possible; predominantly commercial factions—factions, that is, based on economic concerns—are unlikely to be violent. Unlike Bolingbroke, they praised—though with some reservations—the spirit of private interest; they welcomed the fact that Britain had become a predominantly commercial society.

The point that the expansion of commerce breeds nonviolent factions was fully developed by David Hume. Characterizing Bolingbroke's thinking as defective in "argument, method, and precision."[13] Hume argued that Bolingbroke's approach to politics was not only out of touch with the realities of a predominantly commercial society, it was also dangerous to the health of the polity. To adopt Bolingbroke's political rhetoric, Hume suggested, would make political debate difficult, for if each faction argues that it is disinterested, it becomes difficult for factions to work out satisfactory compromises on questions of public policy. In "That Politics May be Reduced to a Science," Hume attacked "zealots on both sides who kindle up the passion of their partisans and, under pretense of public good, pursue the interests and ends of their particular faction."[14] Hume was not asking the different factions to stop pursuing their own interests. Rather, he was asking them to stop pretending that they were working only for the public good. If all factions acknowledged being what Hume called "parties from interest," they would be less likely to fill the nation with "violent animosities." Hume's point is that far from bemoaning the rise of "parties from interest," they should be welcomed, because parties from interest "are the most reasonable and excusable."[15] If such praise seems lukewarm, it is because Hume agreed with Bolingbroke that it would be better if there were no factions. But in a country where liberty exists, Hume said, to strive to achieve a factionless society is simply not practicable. Far better,

[13] Quoted in Garry Wills, *Explaining America* (New York: Doubleday & Co., 1981), p. 22.
[14] Charles W. Hendel, ed., *David Hume's Political Essays* (New York: Liberal Arts Press, 1953), p. 20.
[15] Ibid., p. 80; p. 21.

Hume suggested, to encourage parties from interest rather than what Hume calls "parties from principle"—the latter being factions based on different opinions about religion or government. "Parties from principle" do pose a threat to the health of the polity because they are much less likely to compromise on matters of public policy.

Adam Smith—Hume's disciple and friend—agreed with him about the beneficial political effects of commerce. "The good temper and moderation of contending factions," Smith said in *The Wealth of Nations*, "seems to be the most essential circumstance in the public morals of a free people"; and commerce fosters such moderate, good-tempered factions. Writing about Europe after the fall of the Roman Empire, Smith said: "Commerce and manufactures gradually introduced order and good government, and with them, the liberty and security of individuals, among the inhabitants of the country, who had before lived almost in a continual state of war with their neighbours, and of servile dependency upon their superiors. This, though it has been the least observed, is by far the most important of all their effects. Mr. Hume is the only writer who, so far as I know, has hitherto taken notice of it."[16] Like Hume, Smith thought violent faction was only a remote possibility in Britain precisely because commerce had become so important.

The proponents of a science of politics praised commerce not only for its beneficial political effect but also for its social effect. Commerce, Smith said, enables the poor to better their condition; and "no society can surely be flourishing and happy, of which the far greater part of the members are poor and miserable."[17] Smith and Hume disagreed with those who—like Bolingbroke—looked back in nostalgia to a traditional society. In traditional societies, they argued, the poor are wedded to the land, fit only "for slavery and subjection."[18]

The proponents of a science of politics praised commerce, but they never suggested that Britain should be run by commercial men. Disinterested statesmen—men of enlightened opinions and extensive views—were necessary not only to foster commerce but also to find ways of mitigating some of its harmful effects. The scientists of politics, in fact, were suspicious of commercial men. Smith is wrongly regarded both by those who praise him and by those who damn him as someone who thought that the self-interest of commercial man is an unqualified force for the good. By no means did

[16] *The Wealth of Nations*, ed. Edwin Canaan (New York: Random House, 1937), p. 729, p. 385.

[17] Ibid., p. 79.

[18] *David Hume's Political Essays*, p. 128.

Smith—or Hume for that matter—regard "the private market as infinitely exact, sensitive, efficient and impartial in its resolution of our social and economic perplexities," as Arthur Schlesinger, Jr., has claimed.[19] Smith was not an advocate of laissez faire; he saw a wide and elastic range of activity for government.

Smith, of course, did praise self-interest: "It is not from the benevolence of the butcher, the brewer, or the baker, that we expect our dinner, but from their regard to their own interest." He also stated that "by pursuing his own interest, [the businessman] frequently promotes that of the society more effectually than when he really intends to promote it." Yet although Smith exhorted legislators to "trust people with the care of their own interest," he also warned legislators to be wary of the schemes people devise to advance their interests: "The interest of the dealers . . . in any particular branch of trade or manufactures, is always in some respects different from, or even opposite to, that of the public." It is always in the interest of such men "to narrow the competition"—that is, to restrict trade in order to maximize profits. Therefore the proposal of any new law or regulation which comes from such men "ought never to be adopted till after having been long and carefully examined."[20]

The dynamics of a predominantly commercial polity seem shot through with contradiction in that Smith categorized self-interest as both in the public interest and against it. Smith tried hard to get around this problem by implying that short-run self-interest is different from long-run self-interest. Restricting commerce, he argued, may be in the short-run interest of merchants and manufacturers, but it is not in their long-run interest insofar as they are consumers as well as producers. That is, mercantilist policies might enable them to make greater profits in their own businesses, but they would also have to pay more for everything they wanted to buy. Thus Smith called their interest in restricting trade "futile" in that restricting trade ultimately does not benefit them. Smith was certain that the "real interests"—that is, the long-run interests—of merchants and manufacturers coincided with the public interest in free trade. He doubted very much, however, that such men would ever come to understand their "real interests," for they were imbued with the "monopolizing spirit" and the "meanness of mercantile prejudice."[21]

Smith, then, did not expect to change the thinking of merchants and manufacturers, but he did hope that his arguments would per-

19 "Is Liberalism Dead?" *New York Times Magazine,* 30 March 1980, p. 71.
20 *Wealth of Nations,* p. 14; p. 423; p. 250.
21 Ibid., pp. 625-626; pp. 604-605.

suade legislators to resist the mercantilist nostrums offered by merchants and manufacturers. The record of legislators, Smith argued, had not been very good, for all too often they had allowed the short-run interests of producers to outweigh the long-run interests of producers and consumers alike. *The Wealth of Nations* is a book written primarily for legislators, not for merchants and manufacturers or for scholars of political economy. Only legislators, Smith thought, were sufficiently disinterested to be able to appreciate his arguments. And, of course, only legislators could act upon them. Smith's science of politics aimed at improving society "not by delineating plans of new constitutions, but by enlightening the policy of actual legislators."[22]

Like all the proponents of a science of politics, Smith thought that commerce makes it possible for free governments to avoid violent faction, but he also thought that free governments cannot remain stable without strong legislatures—legislatures composed of men of uncommon abilities. Warning the British Parliament about the dangers of undermining the colonial assemblies in America, Smith said: "Upon the power which the greater part of the leading men, the natural aristocracy of every country, have of preserving or defending their respective importance, depends the stability and duration of every system of free government."[23] One of the prime tasks of such a natural aristocracy, Smith argued, is promoting commerce—a task that often means resisting the pleas of businessmen, who want to restrict commerce.

The Science of Politics in America

The road from Hume and Smith to the authors of *The Federalist* is direct. Although the authors of *The Federalist*, unlike Hume and Smith, supported a republican form of government, all were in favor of a strong national government, one in which legislators would deliberate about the claims of different parties from interest while always keeping in mind the need to foster a progressive economy. *The Wealth of Nations* and *The Federalist*, however, were written with very different purposes in mind. Smith's intention was to persuade a strong national legislature that it should resist the mercantilist schemes of commercial men; the authors of *The Federalist* hoped to persuade delegates to state ratifying conventions to agree to a strong national government. Smith spoke of the beneficial political effects of

[22] Dugald Steward, Smith's first biographer, quoted in Donald Winch, *Adam Smith's Politics* (Cambridge: Cambridge University Press, 1978), pp. 24, 25.
[23] Smith, *Wealth of Nations*, p. 586.

commerce in order to persuade legislators to abjure mercantilism, which impedes commerce. The authors of *The Federalist* spoke of the beneficial political effects of commerce in order to persuade the delegates that a strong national government would not—in a predominantly commercial polity—subvert their liberty.

As many historians have pointed out, the authors of *The Federalist* faced a difficult task because Americans, much more than Englishmen, were generally suspicious of political authority. In Britain many people had grown weary of Bolingbroke's "patriotic" approach to politics; in the American colonies, however, the ideas of Bolingbroke had always been taken seriously; the ideas of Bolingbroke and like-minded writers shaped the mind of the American revolutionary generation.[24]

After the Revolution, many Americans—alarmed by the increasing disorders of the Confederation—denounced private interest and called for a renewal of civic virture. By the 1780s, however, Madison and Hamilton had begun to realize that attacks on the spirit of private interest and calls for civic virtue were not effective prescriptions for the disorders of the Confederation. "We may preach," Hamilton said in 1782, "till we are tired of the theme, the necessity of disinterestedness in republics, without making a single proselyte. The virtuous declaimer will neither persuade himself nor any other person to be content with a double mess of porridge, instead of a reasonable stipend for his services."[25] Not only was it impractical to expect to transform Americans into disinterested citizens, it was also foolish to assume that Americans would ever agree about most political questions. The "patriotic" approach to politics, Madison argued in *The Federalist*, was appropriate only during the years of the Revolutionary War, when the external danger gave the people "an enthusiastic confidence . . . in their patriotic leaders, which stifled the ordinary diversity of opinions on great national questions."[26] Like Hume and Smith, Madison assumed that factions are inevitable in a polity where liberty flourishes, and therefore that a "patriotic" approach to politics —in which each faction proclaims that it is disinterested—is dangerously divisive. Persuading the delegates to the state ratifying convention that a "patriotic" approach to politics was foolish, however, was not the only goal of the authors of *The Federalist*. They also wanted to persuade the delegates that the expansion of commerce in the new

---

[24] See Bernard Bailyn, *The Ideological Origins of the American Revolution* (Cambridge: Harvard University Press).

[25] Hamilton, *Basic Ideas*, p. 69.

[26] *The Federalist*, no. 49, p. 315.

republic would breed so many factions that no one faction would predominate—thereby removing the danger of majority faction. Finally, they hoped to persuade the delegates that because these factions were parties from interest, not principle, the growth of factions would not lead to civil discord.

Yet in *Federalist* 10, Madison seems to imply that factions are dangerous to the health of the polity. People have a "zeal for different opinions," and their zeal is such that they continually look for reasons to join factions—even dream up reasons. "So strong is this propensity of mankind to fall into mutual animosities that where no substantial occasion presents itself the most frivolous and fanciful distinctions have been sufficient to kindle their unfriendly passions and excite their most violent conflicts."[27] If it is true that factions (Madison spoke of parties, using Hume's word) are "much more disposed to vex and oppress each other than to co-operate for their common good," then how is republican government—or any free government, for that matter—possible?

Madison's answer was the same as Hume's and Smith's. After speaking of the tendency of mankind to gravitate toward violent conflicts, Madison began the next sentence with an important "but": "But the most common and durable source of factions has been the various and unequal distribution of property." The "but" implies that Madison regarded property-based factions as somewhat different from those factions he had just discussed. Factions based on differences of property also can result in violent civil discord, but they are less likely to do so in "civilized nations"—that is, in predominantly commercial nations. In such nations, there are not two distinct interests—the propertied and the propertyless—but many. "A landed interest, a manufacturing interest, a mercantile interest, a moneyed interest, with many lesser interests, grow up of necessity in civilized nations, and divide them into different classes, actuated by different sentiments and views." Madison's clear implication was that factions based on different interests are less likely to be zealous—less likely to vex and oppress each other—than factions based on different opinions about religion and government. Factions based on different interests can be regulated: "The regulation of these various and interfering interests forms the principal task of modern legislation and involves the spirit of party and faction in the necessary and ordinary operations of government."[28] The key word is "modern": Such interests only exist in modern—that is, predominantly commercial—polities. The

---

[27] *The Federalist*, no. 10, p. 79.
[28] Ibid.

expansion of commerce not only makes a "patriotic" politics impracticable, it also helps to reduce the likelihood of violent factional discord.

The authors of *The Federalist*, however, did not rule out the possibility that factions based on opinion—what Hume calls parties from principle—would arise, even though America was becoming a commercial society. They hoped that by extending the sphere of government, the damage such factions could do would be limited. "The influence of factious leaders," Madison said in *Federalist* 10, "may kindle a flame within their particular States but will be unable to spread a general conflagration through the other States."[29]

The chief reason the authors of *The Federalist* wanted to extend the sphere of government, however, was their hope that doing so would lead to the creation of a national legislature composed of "men who possess the most attractive merit and the most diffusive and established characters." Hamilton thought it was foolish to preach the necessity of disinterestedness in republics, but both he and Madison thought the new scheme of government would be better than the Confederation because the nation would be more likely to be governed by men of "enlightened views and virtuous sentiments"—by men, that is, who would be animated by a disinterested concern for the health of the nation.[30]

Such men would not be more moral than other Americans. They too would be animated by self-interest, but their self-interest would take the form of political ambition rather than commercial ambition—a desire less to better their condition than to gain fame as legislators. Those writers who subscribed to a "patriotic" approach to politics generally looked with disfavor on political ambition; they thought it inherently corrupting. By contrast, the authors of *The Federalist* in general considered political ambition a force for the good. Of course, they acknowledged that some men might be corrupted by power—Madison in *Federalist* 51 said that "ambition must be made to counteract ambition"—but they also thought that many would be elevated by the responsibility of holding office. By virtue of sitting in a national legislature, they would become "superior to local prejudices."[31] Legislators might begin their terms of office regarding themselves primarily as spokesmen for the interests of their constituents, but many would eventually come to realize that the safety and prosperity of the nation required that they take a more extensive view of public

[29] Ibid., p. 84.
[30] Ibid., p. 83; pp. 83-84.
[31] *The Federalist*, no. 51, p. 84.

questions. Many would come to realize, furthermore, that the interests of their constituents might at times have to be sacrificed to the necessities of this larger view. The authors of *The Federalist* hoped that a national legislature would generate a collegial spirit that would make legislators closer to each other in many respects than to their constituents. Disinterestedness, one might say, was something one gained by virtue of being a national legislator.

Politics and Economics

The authors of *The Federalist*, then, thought that a strong national government was necessary for the health of the republic—necessary but not sufficient; political stability would be undermined if commerce did not expand. "The prosperity of commerce," Hamilton said in *Federalist* 12, "is now perceived and acknowledged by all enlightened statesmen to be the most useful as well as the most productive source of national wealth, and has accordingly become a primary object of their political cares."[32] The prosperity of commerce, however, did not simply happen; it had to be fostered by legislators. Believing that a polity is healthy insofar as it has a progressive economy, and that an economy is most likely to be progressive if trade is not restricted, the authors of *The Federalist* were generally in favor of free trade. Yet occasions were bound to arise when trade would have to be restricted, and legislators were in the best position to know when the public interest required this. The authors of *The Federalist* praised commerce for its beneficial political effects, so they certainly would have had no compunction about restricting commerce if they thought the overall health of the polity dictated it. The authors of *The Federalist* did not think of the economic world as a territory distinct from the political world. A progressive economy can only exist, they assumed, within a strong and stable polity. They believed it was essential that the economic life of the nation be regulated by national legislators— especially because commercial men, concerned with bettering their condition, would tend to neglect the question of national security. "If we mean to be a commercial people," Hamilton says in *Federalist* 34, "it must form a part of our policy to be able one day to defend that commerce."[33]

The subtle relationship of polity to economy in the thought of the authors of *The Federalist* can be gleaned from other writings of

[32] *The Federalist*, no. 12, p. 91.
[33] *The Federalist*, no. 34, p. 208.

Madison and Hamilton. "In all doubtful cases," Madison once wrote, "it becomes every Government to lean rather to a confidence in the judgment of individuals, than to interpositions controlling the free exercise of it." The government, Madison implied in the same letter, should have a disposition in favor of the free market; but he went on to say that there are times when the theory of "let us alone" (laissez faire) is inappropriate. He concluded that the power granted to Congress to regulate commerce was "properly granted, inasmuch as power is, in effect, confined to that body, and may, when exercised with a sound legislative discretion, provide the better for the safety and prosperity of the nation."[34]

Hamilton's view of laissez faire was similar. "This favorite dogma," he said, "when taken as a general rule, is true . . . [but] as an exclusive one, it is false, and leads to error in the administration of public affairs."[35] According to both Hamilton and Madison, the health of the polity required that the economic world be subject to regulation by the political world. Only a strong national government could promote the prosperity of the nation by making sure that commercial men did not strangle competition; only a strong national government could ensure the safety of the nation by attending to questions of foreign and defense policy. Finally, only a strong national government could promote the health of the polity by finding ways of mitigating the bad effects of commercial expansion. "The vigor of government," Hamilton said, "is essential to the security of liberty."[36]

The Nineteenth Century and Economic Freedom

Unfortunately, the nineteenth-century defenders of capitalism abandoned the concept of political economy held by the eighteenth-century defenders of commerce. Although the defenders of capitalism also spoke of the science of political economy, they generally had an inflexible notion of what "science" means. Swearing allegiance to laissez faire, they spoke of inviolable laws—arguing that if these laws were tampered with not only would the economy be ruined but liberty would be undermined. Many of the most inflexible champions of laissez faire were high-minded intellectuals and political reformers such as E. L. Godkin, the editor of *The Nation*, and William Graham

[34] Marvin Meyers, ed., *The Mind of the Founder: Sources of the Political Thought of James Madison* (New York: Bobbs-Merrill, 1973), pp. 483, 485.

[35] Quoted in *Alexander Hamilton and the Founding of the Nation*, ed. Richard B. Morris (New York: Dial Press, 1957), p. 335.

[36] *The Federalist*, no. 15, p. 35.

Sumner, a professor of social theory at Yale. In the opinion of these nineteenth-century "liberals," the economy should not be interfered with; they attacked businessmen for asking favors from government almost as vigorously as they attacked supposedly corrupt politicians.

During the past hundred years, the language of political discourse has changed, so that now those who look with disfavor on government intervention in the economy usually are called conservatives; but the arguments of many contemporary American conservatives are very similar to the arguments of many nineteenth-century liberals. Both speak of the close connection between what they call economic liberty—or economic freedom—and political liberty. Summing up and indeed endorsing the views of nineteenth-century liberals, Milton Friedman—a leading American "conservative"—has said that "their emphasis was on economic freedom as a means toward political freedom."[37] And Friedman stressed his agreement with another contemporary "conservative" economist, Friedrich Hayek, who argued in *The Road to Serfdom* that a continued movement toward centralized control of economic activity would undermine political liberty.

The relationship between economic freedom and political freedom, however, is more complex than most contemporary conservatives allow. For one thing, the concept of economic freedom is a relatively vague one, whereas the concept of political freedom is not. "If liberty means anything at all," George Orwell said, "it means the right to tell people what they do not want to hear."[38] Political liberty is bound up with freedom of speech and press. The extent of a regime's commitment to political liberty can also be gauged by seeing whether it has competitive elections, an independent judiciary, habeas corpus, and freedom to emigrate. We can look around the world and decide relatively easily which regimes are devoted to political liberty, but we cannot so easily decide which regimes are devoted to economic liberty—especially since in recent years many Communist regimes have rolled back the public sector, allowing private agriculture, numerous private businesses, even private property, without granting their citizens an iota of political liberty. What constitutes economic freedom has changed during the course of the past century, moreover. During the heyday of classical liberalism, economic freedom meant virtually untrammeled free enterprise, but only doctrinaire libertarians want to return to such a state of affairs. No doubt the changes of the

---

[37] *Capitalism, Socialism, and Democracy: A Symposium Reprinted from Commentary* (Washington, D.C.: American Enterprise Institute, 1979), p. 99.

[38] Quoted in Steven Marcus, "George Orwell," *New York Times Book Review*, 22 March 1981, p. 26.

past hundred years have limited the operations of the market, but have they destroyed economic freedom? It is hard to say, because economic freedom is such a hazy notion.

Finally, the dire predictions of Hayek, Friedman, and other proponents of laissez faire that the growth of government interference in the economy would undermine political freedom have not been borne out. There has been no road to serfdom. In the last hundred years capitalism has transformed itself—if not totally, at least substantially—without undermining political freedom. Countries such as Great Britain or Israel, where the public sector of the economy is very large, have not suffered a diminution of political freedom. Many repressive regimes, moreover, have market-oriented economies; and even Nazi Germany and Fascist Italy, which were totalitarian, allowed a good deal of private enterprise. To speak of economic freedom, then, may be to divert attention from the only real freedom—political freedom. Repressive regimes can contend that although their people may not be free to criticize the ruler or ruling party, they are "free" to own a house or a business. For that matter, what might have happened in the United States if politicians had listened to such intellectuals as Godkin and Sumner and had not passed laws that mitigated the rigors of laissez faire? If economic freedom had been given full sway, the United States might have suffered from violent factional discord that could have led to an erosion of political freedom. It should also be borne in mind that the strongest defenders of political freedom throughout the world have rarely been those who praise economic freedom. In the United States the most vigilant and outspoken defender of political freedom has been the AFL-CIO, an organization that nineteenth-century liberals and many contemporary conservatives have regarded as an impediment to economic freedom.

The authors of *The Federalist* would not have refrained from supporting government policies that restricted the operations of the market in order to preserve liberty. It cannot be said that they would have approved of unions or the vast increase in government regulation in the 1960s and 1970s, but it can be said that they would not have disapproved of these changes in principle. Still, even if economic freedom is a misleading and possibly insidious term, is there not a point at which government intervention in the economy does begin to erode political freedom? If the state becomes the dominant employer, it may have an inhibiting effect on liberty; people may be afraid to speak out for fear of losing their jobs. The Soviet constitution says that everyone has a right to a job, but dissidents find it impossible to get jobs and often are prosecuted for "parasitism."

According to Leszek Kolakowski, a society in which the state is the sole employer is necessarily totalitarian. "As long as large numbers of people exist whose livelihood and conduct of life are independent from the state, your tyranny—hard and bloodthirsty though it may be—cannot be totalitarian." [39] On the other hand, even a society with a completely state-run economy might preserve liberty, given an independent judiciary, a free press, and competitive elections. Yet if such a polity is theoretically possible, it has never existed and probably never will, for it is highly unlikely that a party which ran for office on a platform of total state control of the economy would ever win an election.

To question the concept of economic freedom, however, is not to deny the many virtues of private enterprise. Extensive government control of the economy, as observers both on the Left and the Right have said recently, inhibits entrepreneurial activity and results in economic stagnation. The authors of *The Federalist* thought that economic growth was essential to the stability of the polity, and they thought it could take place only in a society in which most of the decisions about employment and the allocation of capital were made by private citizens. They did not, however, look upon government interference in the economy as necessarily a force that hampered productivity. There were many things government could do to abet commercial prosperity, and in fact the American government has done much to stimulate American productivity—especially by aiding in the creation of a complex and generally efficient system of national transportation.

Economic Equality

If the authors of *The Federalist* would have questioned the notion of economic freedom, they would also have questioned the notion of economic equality. The attempt to level out economic differences would certainly undermine what Hamilton called "the prosperity of commerce" and thus ultimately increase the possibility of factional discord. Recently, however, economic equality has become a rallying cry for many democratic socialists who have backed away from the idea that nationalization is the main component of socialism and begun to argue that one of the central tenets of socialism is the promotion of economic equality.

According to Michael Walzer, promoting economic equality means pushing for "a radical redistribution of wealth." The current distribu-

[39] "The Devil in History," *Encounter*, vol. 56, no. 1 (January 1981), p. 13.

tion, he says, is unfair because "money . . . enables the men and women who possess it to purchase every other sort of social good." No doubt he is right to say that rich people usually get better services for themselves than poor people—better health care, better legal advice, even better education for their children. Walzer also says that money enables people to buy political power, though he offers no evidence to support this contention. He is not content, however, with saying that we should find ways of providing better services for the poor. What socialists want, he says, is *"the abolition of the power of money outside its sphere.* What socialists want is a society in which wealth is no longer convertible into social goods with which it has no intrinsic connection."[40]

But what does it mean to say that the power of money should be abolished "outside its sphere"? What is the "sphere" of money? Money has no intrinsic value; its only significance is what Walzer calls its "exchange value." A society in which money is no longer convertible into social goods with which it has no intrinsic connection is a society in which social goods come to those who have the right political connections—who are members of the ruling party or have friends in high places. In such societies the power of money is never completely abolished; it comes in, so to speak, through the back door. In such societies, people get the social goods they want by means of bribery and the black market. One need not be a devotee of economic freedom to realize that the ability to make money and spend it the way one wants makes it less likely that one will be subservient to the state—less likely that one will be afraid to speak out and criticize those in power.

The attempt of the government to redistribute wealth would probably lead to a tremendous growth in black market activity and it also would increase other forms of corruption. Such a project, moreover, would undermine the health of the regime because it would undermine the commercial ambition of the American people. According to John Adams, "there is no people on earth so ambitious as the people of America"—ambitious to better their conditon, ambitious to achieve commercial success. And this ambition, Adams said, makes them "sober, industrious, and frugal."[41] By drastically limiting the rewards of commercial success, democratic socialists would thwart this ambition. The economy would suffer, but so too might the American character. For in such a state, "the assiduous merchant, the

---

[40] *Radical Principles* (New York: Basic Books, 1980), p. 240; p. 248.
[41] Quoted in Ralph Lerner, "Commerce and Character: The Anglo-American as New-Model Man," *William and Mary Quarterly*, vol. 36 (January 1979), p. 17.

laborious husbandman, the active mechanic, and the industrious manufacturer" would no longer look forward, as Hamilton said in *Federalist* 12, "with eager expectation and growing alacrity to this pleasing reward [that is, money] of their toils."[42] If a radical redistribution of wealth took place, the industrious American man of commerce might first become apathetic, then cynical, and finally embittered that he was not enjoying the reward of his toils.

Walzer, however, seems less disturbed by the unequal distribution of wealth than by the realization that "the present distribution of wealth makes no moral sense." Capitalism, he argues, is inherently unfair because it does not recognize the "intrinsic value" of work or the "individual qualities" of the worker.[43] Capitalism pays no attention to what we might call the essential nature of things.

But how do we pay attention to the essential nature of things? When Samuel Johnson was asked whether merit ought to make the only distinction among mankind, he replied, "Why, Sir, mankind have found that this cannot be. How shall we determine the proportion of intrinsic merit? Were that to be the only distinction amongst mankind, we should soon quarrel about the degrees of it."[44] Just as Johnson questioned the rationalist assumption that disinterested people can come to agreement about someone's intrinsic merit, he would surely question Walzer's assumption that disinterested people can devise a formula whereby wealth would be distributed according to intrinsic merit. Such a project is unlikely to be attempted, but if it were it would increase the likelihood of factional discord. For Americans would naturally question the basis for such judgments, and certainly those deemed less meritorious than others would resent such a judgment. Walzer does not realize that it is precisely because most Americans do not think the present distribution of wealth makes any moral sense that they are inclined to accept it. Americans may think rich people are smarter, better looking, more ambitious, more energetic, or simply luckier than poor people. They do not, however, think that rich people are better than poor people. The more government interferes in the distribution of wealth, the more people are inclined to become indignant about not having been awarded a "fair" share of the rewards. Thus the attempt to implement economic equality would erode political freedom because it would tend to create

---

[42] *The Federalist*, no. 12, p. 91.

[43] Walzer, *Radical Principles*, p. 255; p. 249.

[44] Boswell, *Life of Johnson*, ed. R. W. Chapman (London: Oxford University Press, 1970), pp. 312-313.

factional discord and increase distrust in the workings of the American form of representative government.

Concerned as they were with ensuring the stability of the American republic, the authors of *The Federalist* would have questioned the wisdom of pursuing either economic freedom or economic equality. Would they not also have questioned the wisdom of continually resorting to such terms as "capitalism" and "socialism" when discussing the nature of the American regime? In his first inaugural address, Jefferson said that "we are all Republicans, we are all Federalists." In a sense we are all socialists insofar as even self-described capitalists do not want to return to the untrammeled capitalism that nineteenth-century liberals advocated. And in a sense we are all capitalists insofar as even self-described socialists do not want to abolish private property or private enterprise. Classical socialism—the socialism of Marx and Lenin—has been repudiated by most intellectuals, although a few adherents still exist on college campuses. And classical capitalism—the capitalism of Godkin and Sumner—has been repudiated by most intellectuals as well.

The political economy of the eighteenth-century scientists of politics, I would argue, is more relevant to our present discontents than either the political economy of the nineteenth-century liberals, with their rigid faith in the supposedly scientific laws of economics, or the political economy of nineteenth-century socialists, with their rigid faith in the supposedly scientific laws of historical development. By looking back at *The Federalist*, then, we can move beyond such notions as capitalism and socialism toward the realization that a market economy is most conducive to the stability of the American polity. The essential subject of debate, then, should be ways of fostering commercial growth while both ensuring the safety of the nation and providing for those who—for whatever reason—have not been able to provide for themselves. Or, to put it another way, the essential concern is to determine the proportion and limits of public and private control that will best ensure the safety and prosperity of the nation.

The Task of Legislators

It is misguided to assume, however, that the boundaries of the public sector can remain fixed; they will always change with changing circumstances. Making the necessary adjustments, the authors of *The Federalist* knew, is not a task for economic experts but for wise legislators—men not blinded by temporary or partial considerations, men who recognize what George Will has called "the dignity of the political vocation and the grandeur of its responsibilities."[45] As Madison says in *Federalist* 57, "the aim of every political constitution is, or ought to be, first to obtain for rulers men who possess most wisdom to discern, and most virtue to pursue, the common good of the society."[46]

Have such enlightened and disinterested men predominated in Congress? Most Americans would say no. Americans have always been suspicious of national legislators, assuming that sooner or later they are corrupted by power. In the eighteenth century this corrosive suspicion was called jealousy, and in *Federalist* 55 Madison attacked "indiscriminate and unbounded jealousy" as a force that was ultimately destructive of representative government.[47] For the past two hundred years, however, Congress has functioned reasonably well even though many Americans have regarded it as an institution full of venal men. Political jealousy did not undermine the framers' scheme of government because until recently the government did not loom large in most people's lives. Pursuing their self-interest, many Americans were indifferent to the doings of government. During the past fifty years, however, Congress has enacted legislation that has vastly increased the scope of the federal government's concerns. As a result, a vastly increased number of Americans are very much interested in what government does—interested because their interests are directly affected by government programs. This increased interest in government affairs puts a great burden on Congress, in that many Americans invariably regard any change in any program as a sign of either the heartlessness of Congress or its venality. Far from creating trust in government, the expansion of the concerns of government has bred distrust and resentment. According to a recent poll, only 18 percent of the American public have confidence in Congress; and another recent poll has found that approximately two-thirds of the country want to limit the tenure of senators and representatives to twelve years.[48] The more such political jealousy increases, the more calls there will be—from both the Left and the Right—for populist measures of decision making that will weaken the ability of Congress to carry out its intended functions.

[45] George F. Will, *The Pursuit of Happiness and Other Sobering Thoughts* (New York: Harper & Row, 1978), p. xvi.
[46] *The Federalist*, no. 57, p. 350.
[47] *The Federalist*, no. 55, p. 345.
[48] *Public Opinion*, vol. 3, no. 1 (December/January 1980), p. 20; *Washington Post*, 22 April 1981.

If Americans have lost faith in the American form of representative government, what other means do we have of promoting the safety and prosperity of the nation? Surely invoking such notions as capitalism and socialism will not help us address the present discontents. Michael Walzer speaks of "the socialist's faith," yet what faith can we have in socialism when under its banner men have instituted some of the worst tyrannies that have ever existed? George Gilder, a disciple of Milton Friedman, associates faith and capitalism: "Faith in man, faith in the future, faith in the rising returns of giving, faith in the mutual benefits of trade, faith in the providence of God are all essential to successful capitalism."[49] Well-versed in the dismal realities of history, the eighteenth-century scientists of politics— among whom we include the authors of *The Federalist*—would have questioned the basis for such faith. Yet they were moderately hopeful about the future of predominantly commercial societies—hopeful because they thought the expansion of commerce would reduce the possibility of violent civil discord. What they would have questioned is the primacy given to economic prescriptions by the defenders of capitalism. "Commerce and manufactures," Adam Smith said, "can seldom flourish in any state in which there is not a certain degree of confidence in the justice of government."[50] It was not a faith in capitalism that enabled the United States to weather the Great Depression without suffering the fate that befell Germany; it was a faith—vague and at times beset with cynicism and doubt—in the justice of the American form of representative government. If legislators had heeded the advice of either the defenders of laissez faire or the proponents of socialism, they probably would have instigated a full-fledged political crisis. The present discontents are best dealt with not by following the nostrums of "jealous" populists or radical intellectuals, and not by bowing down before the altars of either economic freedom or economic equality, but by pondering the subtle political economy of the authors of *The Federalist*. Madison, Hamilton, and Jay were obviously not socialists, but neither were they capitalists; they were men who hoped that their political economy would make it more likely that Americans would be orderly, temperate, and moderate—and thus make it more likely that the new American republic would survive.

[49] *Wealth and Poverty* (New York: Basic Books, 1981), p. 73.
[50] *Wealth of Nations*, p. 862.

The Editors and the Authors

ROBERT A. GOLDWIN is a resident scholar and director of constitutional studies at the American Enterprise Institute. He served in the White House as special consultant to the president and, concurrently, as adviser to the secretary of defense. He taught at the University of Chicago and Kenyon College and was the dean of St. John's College in Annapolis. His edited books include *How Democratic Is the Constitution?*; *Left, Right and Center*; and *Political Parties in the Eighties*.

WILLIAM A. SCHAMBRA is assistant director of constitutional studies at the American Enterprise Institute and was coeditor of *How Democratic Is the Constitution?* He is editing a collection of essays by the late Martin Diamond.

WALTER DEAN BURNHAM is a professor of political science at Massachusetts Institute of Technology. He is the author of *Critical Elections and the Mainsprings of American Politics*, *The American Party System*, and *Presidential Ballots, 1836–1892*, along with many articles on party politics and political systems.

EDWARD S. GREENBERG is a professor in the Department of Political Science and the Institute of Behavioral Science at the University of Colorado. He is the author of *Serving the Few: Corporate Capitalism and the Bias of Government Policy* and *The American Political System: A Radical Approach*.

ROBERT LEKACHMAN is a professor of economics at the City University of New York. He is the author of *A History of Economic Ideas*, *The Age of Keynes*, and *National Income and the Public Welfare*, and other books and articles on economic theory and politics. He is also a columnist for *Dissent* magazine.

FORREST MCDONALD is a professor of history at the University of Alabama and a Distinguished Senior Fellow, Center for the Study of Southern History and Culture. He is the author of *We the People: The Economic Origins of the Constitution.* He received the Fraunces Tavern Book Award in 1980 for *Alexander Hamilton: A Biography.*

STEPHEN MILLER is a resident fellow at the American Enterprise Institute. He is the author of "Adam Smith and the Commercial Republic," "The Poverty of Socialist Thought," and other articles appearing in *The American Spectator* and *Commentary.* He has taught English at Fairleigh Dickinson University, Rutgers, and Beaver College.

MARC F. PLATTNER is an adviser to the United States mission to the United Nations. He formerly was managing editor and currently is a consulting editor of *The Public Interest* magazine. He served as director of issues research for the Moynihan for Senate campaign in 1976. His writings on economic and political issues include "The Welfare State vs. the Redistributive State," and *Rousseau's State of Nature.*

BERNARD H. SIEGAN is a professor at the University of San Diego Law School. He is the editor of *The Interaction of Economics and the Law; Regulation, Economics and the Law;* and *Government, Regulation and the Economy;* and is the author of two books and numerous articles on zoning and land use regulation.

A Note on the Book

The typeface used for the text of this book is
Palatino, designed by Hermann Zapf.
The type was set by
Hendricks-Miller Typographic Company, of Washington, D.C.
Thomson-Shore, Inc., of Dexter, Michigan, printed
and bound the book, using Warren's Olde Style paper.
The cover and format were designed by Pat Taylor.
The manuscript was edited by Carol Verburg, and
by Margaret Seawell of the AEI Publications staff.

Selected AEI Publications

Public Opinion, published bimonthly (one year, $18; two years, $34; single copy, $3.50)

How Democratic Is the Constitution? Robert A. Goldwin and William A. Schambra, eds. (150 pp., paper $5.25, cloth $12.25)

The Dream of Christian Socialism: An Essay on Its European Origins, Bernarch Murchland (74 pp., $4.25)

Canada at the Polls, 1979 and 1980: A Study of the General Elections, Howard R. Penniman, ed. (426 pp., paper $9.25, cloth $17.25)

The Role of the Legislature in Western Democracies, Norman J. Ornstein, ed. (192 pp., paper $7.25, cloth $15.25)

Liberation South, Liberation North, Michael Novak, ed. (99 pp., $4.25)

British Political Finance, 1830-1980, Michael Pinto-Duschinsky (339 pp., paper $10.50, cloth $17.95)

A Conversation with Michael Novak and Richard Schifter: Human Rights and the United Nations (25 pp., $2.25)

Reconciliation and the Congressional Budget Process, Allen Schick (47 pp., $4.25)

Whom Do Judges Represent? John Charles Daly, mod. (31 pp., $3.75)

Prices subject to change without notice.

AEI Associates Program

The American Enterprise Institute invites your participation in the competition of ideas through its AEI Associates Program. This program has two objectives:

The first is to broaden the distribution of AEI studies, conferences, forums, and reviews, and thereby to extend public familiarity with the issues. AEI Associates receive regular information on AEI research and programs, and they can order publications and cassettes at a savings.

The second objective is to increase the research activity of the American Enterprise Institute and the dissemination of its published materials to policy makers, the academic community, journalists, and others who help shape public attitudes. Your contribution, which in most cases is partly tax deductible, will help ensure that decision makers have the benefit of scholarly research on the practical options to be considered before programs are formulated. The issues studied by AEI include:

- Defense Policy
- Economic Policy
- Energy Policy
- Foreign Policy
- Government Regulation

- Health Policy
- Legal Policy
- Political and Social Processes
- Social Security and Retirement Policy
- Tax Policy

For more information, write to:

AMERICAN ENTERPRISE INSTITUTE
1150 Seventeenth Street, N.W.
Washington, D.C. 20036